CHASING
RELEVANCE

CHASING RELEVANCE

6 STEPS TO UNDERSTAND,
ENGAGE, AND MAXIMIZE
NEXT-GENERATION
~~MILLENNIAL~~
LEADERS IN THE WORKPLACE

Dan Negroni

with Jim Eber

launchb**x

Published by launchbox, Inc.
11839 Sorrento Valley Road, #908
San Diego, CA 92121
www.launchbox365.com

FIRST EDITION: 2016

Library of Congress Cataloging-in-Publication Data is available upon request.

ISBN: 978-0-692-64325-9

Manufactured in the United States of America by RR Donnelley

10   9   8   7   6   5   4   3   2   1

To the mentor inside each of us,
willing to do the work to create
next-generation leaders.

Contents

Origin Story

Soon after starting his first job as a trader in New York City, my son Zach was interrogated at our house in San Diego. Not by the SEC, but by our family friend Rory. A reporter for thirty years, Rory had forged the perfect career for her innate curiosity. Given that inquisitiveness and how much she loves Zach, she simply needed to know more about his job. She cornered him with questions, pushing him for bigger answers about his life.

"What does it mean you are 'in sales and trading' in New York? What do you do? Tell me exactly what you *do*."

Zach finally gave in: "Rory, I do whatever they ask me to do. That's what I do. They want breakfast? I get breakfast. They want shirts from Bloomingdale's? I get shirts from Bloomingdale's. They want their cars out of the garage next door? I take them out. I answer the phone. I do a call for coffee. I develop spreadsheets. I do research. I make a trade. I do whatever they want me to do."

My son, the millennial: Doesn't he sound exactly like what you want in an employee? Don't you wish there were more millennials out there like him doing what they are told? Even if he knew some of the work was menial—even if he didn't love his job—he was willing to grind it out and be the best employee he could be. He was serving time so he could make the climb. That's the correct attitude!

And I am proud of my son. Zach is a hustler. He is a straight-up entrepreneur who always wanted to go to business school and was drawn to international finance. When he graduated from Boston College's Carroll

School of Business, I coached him and his friends, preparing them for interviews, helping them know how to act in the "real world" after college, and focusing on the skills they would need to succeed to get a job. This was nothing new for Zach and me. I have coached him since he was two. It has been a fundamental part of our relationship and who I am as a parent—to be there as a role model, coach, dad, sounding board . . . whatever any of my three children need to succeed and to thrive on their own terms, because I did not have any of that growing up. But Zach was the first of my children to graduate from college and thus the first chance I had to be Coach Dad on the professional ball field. And it had seemingly worked. Now he was the kind of employee who was willing to do whatever it takes to get the job done and overdeliver on expectations for anything and everything, including getting shirts from Bloomingdale's.

I should be proud, right? But Zach sounded *wrong* to me. Something big was missing in his answers to Rory's questions: himself.

I wanted to hear the Zach I knew. To me he did not sound like the best employee *he* could be. He sounded like he was a gofer. That was not Zach. The Zach I knew wanted to grow and learn from the people around him—to stand for and be a real part of something. He wasn't. I heard his annoyance and frustration. He was *done*. He wanted more and he was going to get it. So I started coaching Zach again: teaching, learning, forcing him to tell his story and listening to the answers to help him get what he wanted.

The good news for Zach was that working with him and his friends to find those first jobs had made me a better coach, mentor, and consultant and pushed me to find myself in new ways. It had informed our mission at my new company, launchbox: to help millennials thrive in the workplace, design their lives, connect, feel confident, and communicate their value and purpose. Since then, my work at launchbox has shown me just how much even really smart millennials require continued guidance or "adult supervision" once they land. They need coaches and managers who understand who they are and can help them take control of their situations to deliver results for the company and themselves.

Thus my approach with Zach was no different than with other smart millennials. First, I focused on his personal accountability. I explained to him "what happens to you is because of you" so if he didn't do anything about his work situation, he was just going to keep suffering professionally *and* personally. Then, I pushed him to step back, look around his office, and ask, "Are these the guys I really want to be around? Is it worth it to get in at 6:00 a.m. and work my butt off just to be called a douchebag for my efforts? Is this what I want? *Can* I—and *do* I—want to learn from these guys?"

His answer was, "No."

"Great!" I told him, "Now stop whining and do something about it. This is your life. Shut up and own it."

And he did. He looked for new jobs with a more entrepreneurial bent. As he looked, even though he was unable to find the right opportunities at his current company, he did not abdicate responsibility and accountability to his employers or himself. Once he decided his next step, he quit with a gold star by his name, having excelled at every last task. By the time he was ready to leave, they wanted him to stay, but he told his bosses, "It's about me. I don't want to be a trader. I want to be more entrepreneurial in what I do." Now I was really proud of my son.

If you think I am blind to the fact that Zach was selling his employers a line, I'm not. It *was* him. Zach wasn't the right employee for them. But it was also them: Zach's managers *had* failed him, but since I couldn't control or help them directly—nor was I asked to—I could only try and stop Zach from failing himself.

As an emotional guy who loves nothing more in this world than his children, it had broken my heart watching what happened to Zach. Truth is, my heart breaks every day for the millennials who come through our office, unappreciated, flailing, and failing—falling through the massive and unparalleled gap between generations. We all want to help, guide, teach, and find relevance in bridging our generational worlds. It is the way it has always been and should be, but the gulf between those worlds is wider than ever.

So I asked myself, *How can I create this relevance? What can I do to create and empower the next generation of leaders? How can I become a leader myself and be the guide and, more importantly, make it stick?*

When I asked these questions, I found what Simon Sinek, in his book *Start with Why: How Great Leaders Inspire Everyone to Take Action,* calls my "why"—my purpose, my cause, my belief, my inspiration to do more. This is something I have known I needed to do since I was young. In spite of—or rather because of—my screwed-up childhood, my story has always been to help people and situations to be better than anyone imagines they could be—empowering them, helping them, pushing them to be their best.

I love what happens at the intersection of youth and experience. It is where our culture has always evolved, and it is a powerful space to inhabit. I had found my mission: to create connected workplaces so we can all be better individually. It became apparent to me with each and every conversation that if I cared that deeply about the way we work, I needed to pivot and expand our work at launchbox to focus on non-millennial leaders and managers and those who just lack a millennial mindset regardless of their age.

I know millennials like Zach have much to learn, but their accountability to this problem goes only so far. I know from working with them just how rarely non-millennials are teaching them the skills they need to succeed in the workplace. Which is why my heart does not break when I see non-millennials in the workplace who just don't get this. I may feel sorry for them but really what I want to do is shake them and say, "Come on, it's our job. It's our responsibility. You know this, especially if you are a parent! Why are you so hesitant on fixing yourself first—and *then* seeing what they have to offer and giving them the opportunities to do what will make them and the business successful?"

That's how I realized the question I needed to solve at launchbox wasn't just "How do I teach the *millennials* to be the employees their managers expect and need to succeed?" We needed to ask and answer different questions: "How can *leaders and managers* of millennials reshape what they're doing, understand millennials better, and bridge the gap between generations in the workplace? How can we find relevance by creating next-generation leaders who provide everyone more value and create more success for the world?"

We can't just "fix" millennials—that only reinforces the gap we've already created. That old-school command-and-control attitude toward youth and inexperience will fail every time. Instead, we must lead in new ways—reconstruct ourselves as better, more genuine and caring leaders. Because if we build better managers (selves), we build better employees. Managers like that could impact more "Zachs" than I ever could. I can work with only a few millennials at a time to help them be more successful; managers lead teams and companies. To hold ourselves accountable for eradicating the gap in workplace expectations, we must all find relevance in bridging the skills gap to create next-generation leaders by

- creating powerful, authentic relationships in the workplace
- promoting behavior that creates a culture of openness, delivering value and shared purpose
- teaching real-deal skills and increasing individual accountability to drive company results

Bridging the gap in this book is not just about getting the generations to work together. It's about what I said before: creating next-generation leaders in millennials as well as teaching current managers how to be better leaders by guiding those millennials and letting them guide us. It's about having everyone be their best self by caring enough to connect— and get results that are sustained! But to get there you must work from the inside out and truly understand how to care in the right ways.

Let me be clear: I said "care." This book is about caring—caring enough to tell the truth, be bold, and confront the hard stuff. Don't worry if you feel like questioning that. I welcome it! I want you to engage with all you got. As you will learn through my story in this book, I am a fighter for individuals. Finding relevance in myself and using it to help others has always been my BHAG (big hairy audacious goal), and today my BHAG, a term coined by Jim Collins and Jerry I. Porras in *Built to Last: Successful Habits of Visionary Companies*, is focused on shaking awake as many people as I can to their need to be and remain relevant personally and professionally to the next generation. I strive to right wrongs and make it happen when it comes to you and your millennials. I will straight out call BS when I hear either side pointing fingers at the other. But while I am expressive and this "carefrontation coaching" style may be perceived by some as a bit excessive, I promise you one thing if you let me push you: I've got your back. My personal brand may always be bold, but it is always in the service of my commitment to each and every person I touch to make a difference—not to make a statement but to make a difference.

Because we need something different.

It's not as though we have had great success with millennials by operating like we have in the past and thinking we are doing it right because "that's the way things have always been." Quite the contrary! For example, I start many keynotes by asking the audience three questions.

- How many of you have never had an issue with understanding the next generation/millennials? (No hands go up.)
- How many of you think—even if you have had issues—you are experts and need no other help in creating or becoming next-generation leaders? (No hands go up.)
- How many of you are caring, real people who want to make connections with others? (Almost all the hands go up.)

Truth is, that's always the way it goes: Few if any raise their hands for the first two questions, and most everyone raises their hands for the third. And that's okay. Because if you answered the third question honestly, this book can help you become more relevant for the next chapter of your life and the world by changing your answers to one and two.

This nation has so much to gain at the convergence of youth and experience. Yet instead of bridging the gap between the two, we are creating more conflict, leaving us all confused and chasing relevance. I don't care if your business is law, high tech, engineering, sales, marketing, consulting, manufacturing, parking, dermatology, real estate, restaurants . . . This is the reality of the common problem faced by the thousands of millennials and non-millennials, be they entry-level employees, managers, supervisors, or executives up to the C-level, as they try to find their relevance, purpose, and connection currency during a time of unique generational confluence in our homes, workplaces, and marketplaces. The tension is palpable. Perhaps more than any other generation, millennials want to find their relevance by connecting work and self in this obsessively self-help-oriented and development-focused world. And we non-millennials find ourselves pushed and challenged by this in every aspect of our personal and professional lives. To succeed, we don't need to fight back; we need to upgrade ourselves like we upgrade our software, phones, and apps. If we don't bridge this gap, our own systems may crash, and this time it will be too late to ask millennials how to reboot them.

So we have a choice: Care more about millennials by pushing ourselves to be better leaders and coaches, or continue to be careless by ignoring and dismissing the generational divide.

The answer is clear: We all need to care more about millennials. Because we love them, we need them, and we want them to succeed.

Introduction

WE HATE THEM, WE LOVE THEM

This is not news: The challenge of parenting, educating, training, mentoring, and guiding young people has been around for thousands of years. Consider this quote.

> *Our youth now love luxury. They have bad manners, contempt for authority; they show disrespect for their elders and love chatter in place of exercise; they no longer rise when elders enter the room; they contradict their parents, chatter before company; gobble up their food and tyrannize their teachers.*

Who do you think said that? George Washington? George Bush? Actually those words are widely attributed to Socrates, almost 2,500 years ago. And unlike so many misattributed quotes, Socrates may have actually said these words; they align with his philosophy. In fact, Socrates' student Plato may even have recorded Socrates saying that *about Plato himself*. What a performance review!

The more things change, the more they stay the same? No. Times have changed, and millennials have changed the game. We are disconnected from the largest generation in human history. Millennials (people born between 1980 and 2000) are about 83 million strong in the United States alone. They are already our employees, clients, and customers—and they spend! It's time for businesses and their leaders to change with the times . . . because we have a big problem.

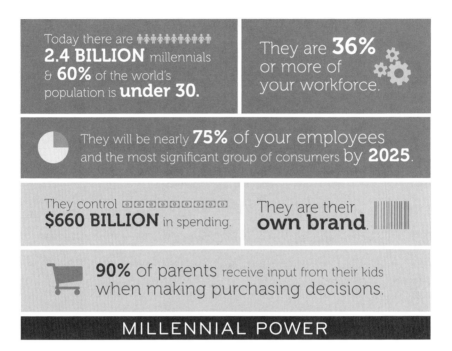

Today there are 2.4 BILLION millennials & 60% of the world's population is under 30.

They are 36% or more of your workforce.

They will be nearly 75% of your employees and the most significant group of consumers by 2025.

They control $660 BILLION in spending.

They are their own brand.

90% of parents receive input from their kids when making purchasing decisions.

MILLENNIAL POWER

A problem that costs businesses more than ever: Our ability to attract, train, manage, and retain this next generation of leaders is critical to the future success of our businesses, but a huge and damaging connection, communication, and understanding gap exists between non-millennials and millennials in our workplaces.

- Thirty percent of organizations lose 15 percent or more of their millennial workforce annually.
- More than 60 percent of millennials leave their employers within three years.
- It costs companies $15,000 to $25,000 to replace each millennial.

A problem that costs employees and businesses.
- Seventy-one percent of organizations report that the loss of millennial employees increased the workload and stress of current employees.

- Workload and stress combine with disconnection to breed disengagement: Seven of ten employees report being "disengaged" or "actively disengaged" at work.
- The estimated cost of this disengagement is $450 *billion*.

A problem that few have a plan for solving.
- Eighty-seven percent of C-suite executives recognize that disengaged employees are among the biggest threats to their businesses.
- Only 22.9 percent of organizations have a plan in place to engage millennials and future generations.

Here is my solution.

- Care more to create genuine connections that compel you and everyone who works with and for you to show up every day accountable to one another and focused on results.
- Work from the inside out to build powerful relationships that bridge the gaps.
- Shift your mindset to one of positive intent, teaching and learning, shared goals, delivering value, and empowering success.

And here's your first step to success: *Stop chasing relevance and find it— get out of your own way and pay attention!*

Yes, you. Everyone.

- **STOP** pointing out problems and saying others are the problem.

- **START** asking yourself, *"What about me is not connecting and getting results? What am I doing to widen and maintain this gap?"*

What I find most curious in dealing with the gap between youth and experience is how put-off and deeply frustrated many leaders from previous generations are by millennials in the workplace, almost as a rule. "Ugh, millennials. I hate them!"

That's all about past allegiances: Managers have been there for a while and are used to doing things their way or the "way things have always been done." (Note: I use "managers," "leaders," and "non-millennials" interchangeably in the book, but millennial managers and leaders who have assimilated the managerial ways of the past are in just as much need of guidance out of those ways.) As a result, they get in their own way when they try to change millennials. And when they inevitably fail? They step all over themselves to blame those millennials and bemoan how "not great" this younger generation is. They paint a completely negative picture of "them," as if millennials are a monolithic group of apathetic, disrespectful, unmanageable brats. They whine about millennials' lack of skills while simultaneously dismissing any value those millennials bring to the table. Millennials are entitled and lazy but they want all the power—all they want is power and all they think about is themselves. They can never become leaders.

"Not true!" you say. "Millennials are great at fixing my devices." Ah, generous praise.

Listen, I get it. The generations in charge right now in business, for the most part, see little value in those millennial qualities in the workplace, and this contaminates their perceptions of millennials as a whole. I see things very differently. I am a proud out-of-the-closet "perennial millen-

GENERATIONAL CONFLICT

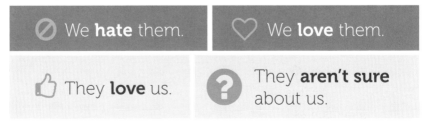

nial"; friends and colleagues today call me "Mr. Millennial." I have all the characteristics of millennials, but I also have the extra time served, which allows me to see both sides of the story and care for them equally.

And this perennial millennial is tired of the intergenerational BS. Because the real deal is much more complicated.

You think millennials want all the power? They *are* the power, and our future. Did you not read those statistics? The sooner you accept this, the better, because how we connect with them in the future will affect everything from sales of toilet paper to cars, where we live, what kind of houses will sell, what kind of energy we use, what kind of food we eat, where we go to school, how we invest and grow savings, teach, where we go on vacation . . . they will eventually define which businesses will make it. As Anne Hubert, senior vice president of Viacom said in her terrific TEDx talk, "[Millennials] decide who will come with them into the future they are building. . . . They decide what to destroy, reinvent, and leave behind."

This is real power, and if we want results in the workplace we need to understand that times have changed. And who was responsible for changing them? These are kids who have been watched over and tracked their entire lives. Tracked. We managed every play date. Recorded every moment. At every step, we gave them "atta girls" and "atta boys," bragged about their cuteness, and babbled about their art, dance, sports, drama, swimming, grades—a trophy or ribbon for everything! We don't want them to fail and never have liked it if they did. To paraphrase Hubert, we were their mammas and paparazzi.

Millennials grew up as their own brands. They grew up "wired" and "wireless" and have never known a world in which technology did not impact, consistently change, and repeatedly shorten timelines of planned obsolescence. They practically Instagrammed their own births and every moment since then. ◗

> Millennials came out of the #womb.

And whose fault is that? Ours. We did it. We made millennials our center of attention as kids and our chief technology officers when they

PROFILE OF A MILLENNIAL

- 📅 Days filled with scheduled activities.
- 🏆 Trophies for everyone on the team.
- 👪 Families of all different shapes and sizes.
- 💬 Socially connected every minute to everyone, everywhere.
- ℹ️ Information at their fingertips.
- 🔀 Multitasking is the norm.
- ◎ Center of attention.
- 💻 Family technologists.

grew up. We gave them a seat at the table and told them to go challenge things. We encouraged them to ask questions. Put it out there. Push. Be better. What's the result? The age-old ideas that experience rules and that time equals experience have forever been confounded. Experience still rules, but experience manifests itself differently today. Given the speed of technological evolution, increasing global openness, and instant availability of information and knowledge, time in this world and on the job is no longer the most predictive indicator of experience.

While that has played out more dramatically in places like Silicon Valley and high-tech businesses, every area of the country and every industry is going to be affected sooner rather than later and thus must learn that the millennial age is upon us; *there is a lot of raw talent out there to attract, coach, teach, and retain.* Fast-growing companies need top millennials to stay with them and grow into great managers and even better leaders than we have been.

"Ugh, really? I hate millennials." Right, I get it. Look at them with their selfies taking pictures of everything they do and then when they are done taking pictures of themselves asking you to take a picture of them . . . right after they answer that Snapchat that just chimed in. And yet . . .

We want to and do *love* them. They are our children. They are innovative and smart and tech savvy. We love the cool they bring. We love their hope and opportunity. We love the energy of their questioning. They disrupt. They challenge. They care about meaning and purpose and balance. They aspire. They inspire. They also love us—they *really* do. We are their parents and grandparents, bosses, and teachers. They want guidance and to learn from us. They see us as equals and rely on us, but . . .

They aren't quite convinced. They may have the power but they also have doubts about us.

And who can blame them? All this conflict is confusing, exhilarating, demanding, and maddening all at the same time. Is it any wonder that they grew up conflicted and anxious? While we raised them, we protected them, told them that they could achieve anything they tried for; as adults, they live in a world of declining opportunity, diminished security, and unprecedented environmental uncertainty. No wonder many millennials are voicing their doubts about us from their parents' homes: According to the US Census Bureau and US Department of Education, almost a third of all millennials lived with their parents during the last recession as many launched careers. Yet even as the US economy improved from 2010 to 2015, according to the Pew Research Center, the share of young adults living in their parents' homes *increased* to 26 percent from 24 percent. Moreover, more than a third of those living independently say they still rely on financial support from their families.

Simply put, many millennials simply can't afford to leave home. They are earning less than eighteen- to thirty-four-year-olds did in 1980. This is the first generation in our country that won't do as well as their parents. It's a time of different wars and different political unrest. It's a time of great divisiveness. Well-paying jobs have been scarce, earnings are stagnant, and as a generation they have accumulated $1.1 trillion in student debt to go with the nation's ongoing budget deficits. Sure, they are more educated, but at what cost? A Huffington Post article by Adam Hanft, "The Stunning Evolution of Millennials: They've Become the Ben Franklin Generation," summed this up perfectly: "[Millennials'] faith in technology is understandable. Algorithms don't act in their own self-interest. Algorithms weren't responsible for dreaming up sub-prime loans and nearly bringing down the financial system. Millennials didn't trust authority and conventional sources of wisdom *before* the meltdown. Imagine now. Wealthfront [an online financial services start-up] argues that Millennials '. . . have been nickel-and-dimed through a wide variety of services, and they value simple, transparent, low-cost services.' The Pew study 'Millennials in Adulthood' confirms the Wealthfront finding that '. . . just 19% of Millennials say most people can be trusted, compared with 31% of Gen Xers, 37% of Silents and 40% of Boomers.' If you can't trust people in general—which was the question—what hope is there for the conniving financial advisor?"

Check out how Levi's (*http://bit.ly/1VblEes*) captures the promise and power of millennials and their aspirational, self-absorbed, conflicted ways in a 2015 commercial. The voiceover starts by telling the millennials dressing and heading down the streets and into offices and classrooms that they are kings and queens and the next real leaders of the world—that they *can* be all that and more. But if you listen to the ad all the way through, the voiceover changes at the end. "Are you joking?" the voice says. "Are you breaking? Are you shaking? You're a kid."

This is the conflict that the power we have given millennials has wrought. They have been told they can be anything—kings and queens, heroes and superstars, entrepreneurs and CEOs—and they expect to be that and more yet they feel scared, insecure, and unworthy. They feel the pressure. Just like us all, they feel doubt, and while they know they have the keys to the kingdom, they may not be ready or quite know what to do with them.

Will they live their dreams? Eighty-four percent of millennials believe they will get where they want, yet 76 percent are unsure and conflicted and are afraid of not living up to their potential and not getting where they need to be. Of course they feel that way. Like that Levi's ad, we've told them that they are kings and queens and "the solo act of the sold-out show of a six-floor stadium." But we haven't really given them the tools to rule or perform. So they are scared. In fact, 39 percent feel they are behind where they want to be.

I see this in my son Zach, who told me recently that he is not sure what he wants to be and where he wants to be. I asked him what he meant, and he told me that his job at a start-up was not making money nor getting him anywhere. He had stopped learning.

"I just feel like I'm a failure," he said.

He felt like a failure? Twenty-three years old and only eighteen months out of school, making 200 cold calls a day, closing deals, at times selling as much as the CEO and delivering real value while he learns. And Zach is the one that thinks he failed even though he delivered? It's shocking, but that's what is going on in the workplace. Come on! We need to help millennials and guide them, because no one else is teaching them otherwise. That is the way it works: They need us and we need them. It's worked this way for generations. Only things are completely different now.

> Who is failing whom?

Problem is, we're not navigating that conflict between the power we have given millennials and their feelings that they may not be ready for it. We're not guiding millennials, sharing our values, and letting them own the power they have to guide themselves. We're asking them to change to fit into our workplaces, because we know what's best. But do we?

As part of our baseline assessments of every client, my team and I use launchbox's proprietary assessment tool, BRIDGEdex, to identify where the significant disconnects exist between millennials and managers—between employee expectations and what they are experiencing in the workplace. We have done hundreds of these assessments with companies of all sizes nationwide, across all industries. Despite the fact that needs differ across departments, disciplines, and industries; despite the fact that sales culture is different from accounting, and practices within law firms or insurance companies are different from engineering or public relations firms; and despite the fact that regional differences exist—San Diego is not the same as Des Moines, which is nothing like New York City—managers' top disconnects and frustrations with their millennials were strikingly similar across all companies regardless of location, size, or industry.

MANAGERS' TOP DISCONNECTS / FRUSTRATIONS WITH THEIR MILLENNIALS

- Lack of initiative / problem-solving
- Sense of entitlement
- Overly self-focused
- Too emotional
- Unrealistic advancement goals
- Impatient
- Inability to remain engaged and loyal
- Poor work ethic
- Not taking responsibility

Of course, these managerial disconnects look exactly like the reasons non-millennials hate millennials. That hate not only creates perceptions and clouds how non-millennial managers view, treat, and lead their millennial employees, but also reveals their biggest—often unknown or unseen—challenges and weaknesses when it comes to understanding millennials.

Because that's the other thing we found: While non-millennials surveyed think they are great at doing the things their millennials need, their millennials decidedly disagree.

MILLENNIALS' TOP DISCONNECTS / FRUSTRATIONS WITH THEIR MANAGERS

- Unavailablity / too busy
- Lack of timely response
- Lack of positive feedback
- Lack of training / development
- Lack of consistent check-ins
- Lack of communication / transparency / consistency
- Ineffective business planning
- Lack of trust

What does this mean? Simply put, if you think you are doing well at something and your audience thinks you are not, that disconnect is not only an organizational problem but also a *personal* problem that you need to solve. If you as an individual can accept all that and own it, you will take the first step in changing your mindset and overcoming disconnects that reveal our biggest weaknesses and challenges in dealing with millennials—and in turn get them to change their mindset about you.

It's not like we don't have some of this "millennials are not the enemy" mindset already. While our popular culture still tilts toward annoying and often cheap stereotypical jokes about the non-millennial-versus-millennial conflict, movies like *The Intern*—starring Robert De Niro and Anne Hathaway and written by a non-millennial—are mining the reality beneath the stereotypes of generational conflict. And it's not like non-millennials don't expect millennials to present themselves differently. NPR did a story about college graduates who had landed jobs talking to seniors at their alma maters. One graduate told the audience that the old black-and-white résumé with twelve-point type just doesn't cut it anymore; she said companies expect an "infographic résumé" linking to a website, a portfolio of work, and a video. Of course, no one from previous generations did this. Yet it is non-millennials at these com-panies who are asking for and expecting these résumés. So we expect millennials to present themselves differently from the moment we meet them, but we don't expect millennials to act differently than the previ-ous generation once they get the job?

Why do we get that millennials as a group do things differently, but ignore the reasons why and/or paint those differences as bad and thus less valuable—as something that stands in the way of results, as some-thing to be changed rather than embraced and channeled into empower-ment, shared goals, and results for the company? Why do we only see "reality" in the movies?

Because millennials push us and challenge what we have come to accept—which is exactly why we want them to change. So we try to change them into us.

After all, non-millennials are not used to being flexible. For decades we haven't even been flexible enough at work to take the vacations we've earned and are entitled to. We claim to want work/life balance yet the US Bureau of Labor Statistics reports that the average American works about one month more a year than in 1976. According to a 2014 Oxford Economics analysis, the average American takes less paid vacation time than at any point in the past four decades—leaving more than eight days unused annually, for a total of 429 million unused days per year nation-wide. In fact, we are the only industrialized nation that doesn't mandate vacations.

For all these reasons and more, according to James Surowiecki in his *New Yorker* article "The Cult of Overwork," "Overwork has become a cre-dential of prosperity." Of course, we will always find workers who are willing to pay that price for prosperity but only because the people in power are charging the admission. "We went through it and so should they!" non-millennials snap. "Why should *I* change my work and the way *I* work for *them*? *I'm* not supposed to change; *they* are."

That's ridiculous. You are already so fantastic at being a leader that they need to change? It's not "us versus them" and "if you're not with us you're against us." How is that working, "us"? *That kind of thinking is what got us into this mess.*

So how do we guide millennials to be their best selves and find their own relevance while still doing the work we need them to do? How will we create alignment between millennials' expectations and what they are experiencing in your workplace?

How do you engage the next generation of employees and customers? What are you going to do?

Nothing? Okay, let me know how that works for you.

> Today's companies need to bridge the gap between their managers' skills and perceptions and millennials' skills and needs in order to create an engaged, productive workplace that delivers results.

Wait and see? Maybe you think millennials are only in high-tech businesses and not in your industry. Or maybe you get it, but you don't see or have the need yet. You're not going to adjust the way your non-millennial employees work to accommodate the few millennials in your business. You're like people who think they don't need insurance because they're healthy. But no business is immune to this problem, and disruptive businesses know it doesn't take long for disruption to become the norm. If they're not your employees, they are or will soon be your customers.

Act? Okay, let's exercise your mentorship muscles and bridge the gap by focusing on some simple principles and committing to the hard work needed to implement them. You're who we created launchbox and wrote this book for, and I promise that in the end you'll be changing your perspective, understanding and caring about millennials, and coaching and working a whole lot better with them, your entire team, and every person close to you in your life.

That's right: The work ahead, just like the work we do at launchbox, has the power to change your life *and* your whole company culture and focus. Albert Einstein said, "A new type of thinking is essential if mankind is to survive and move toward higher levels." I agree. And acting on that thinking starts with your duty to understand yourself—to work from the inside out to be the best leader you can be.

That's why acting to bridge this gap does not begin with a bulleted list of action items. In fact, bridging the gap doesn't even start *in* the workplace. That's Part Two of the book, where we get into communication, training, development, and collaboration. Part One, on working from the inside out, starts by elevating and developing the most important skill in life: the ability to build relationships.

Like the flight attendant says, "Put on your own oxygen mask first before affixing it to your millennial." Okay, they don't say that. I do. But you'll need a clear head and may need oxygen on the journey to relevance and results. Will it be painful? Yes. Different? Completely. Unknown? Absolutely! But as one of my clients said, "You can use these immediately actionable techniques that will improve your company and your culture, or you can just ignore 83 million-plus millennials in the United States and 2.4 billion worldwide."

The choice is ours.

What do you want to do? Create real and personal relevance, impact the world, build your business, increase your client base, own your success path, improve your management skills, create effective sales and marketing programs, become a leader, create effective training or mentoring/coaching programs, measure and track your progress and results, increase your sphere of influence, define your personal brand and story, differentiate yourself from the competition, create more balance in your life, attract or become a mentor . . . ?

Then you need to treat your next-generation leaders like you treat your customers and live it! And mean it! And follow up with it! And coach it! Imagine what the world would look like if we did that. We would be able to soften—or even get rid of—the conflict and create connection and results in the workplace. We'd have alert, peaceful, relaxed, fit, energetic, healthy, successful, hopeful, confident, happy, productive millennials with positive mindsets as opposed to stressed, unfit, insecure, sick, depressed, unproductive employees with negative mindsets.

We know that companies change slowly. We also know that individuals can change quickly to lead from the inside out. Let's launch you out of the box in Part One, and then in Part Two help you build genuine and connected relationships with your people, write new rules for the workplace and marketplace of the future, and win the millennial race.

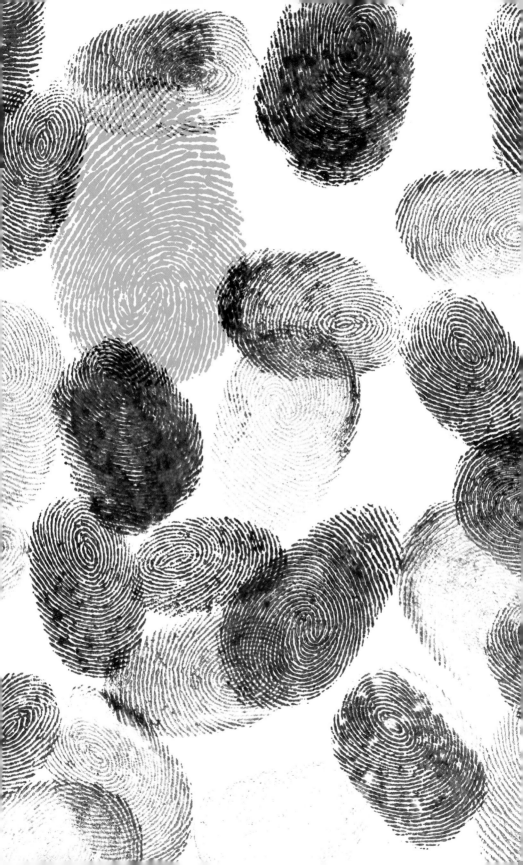

PART ONE
Work from the Inside Out

Focus on where you want to go; not on what you fear.
—Tony Robbins, *Unleash the Power Within*

Our team was presenting to leaders at one of my largest clients when one of the gentlemen in the back who had been with the company for three decades piped in.

"Look," he said, "I had to do it this way. They should have to do it this way. They should just shut their mouths and do it the way I did it. I didn't like my boss for fifteen years and I still did what I was told and . . ." I listened as "Angry John" went on, getting angrier and angrier as he went. I let him go a bit, and then calmly asked him to slow down and take a breath. And then I let him have it in a kind but direct way.

"How does what you did thirty years ago matter today? How is it relevant to anyone but you?"

He looked at me. He still looked tense. I continued.

"I don't deny what you went through, but why do you want the same for them? We are talking about the present—today—and what we want to create for the future. What is what you did thirty years ago, when there were no mobile phones and you weren't getting hundreds of texts a day, have to do with today and tomorrow?"

The room fell silent as Angry John looked at me and said, "I guess not much."

Good guess. Great start to getting out of his own way and moving forward.

Let's be honest: What stands in the way of change are people, and too many leaders don't include themselves as "people" complicit, let alone responsible for, the gaps between millennials and non-millennials in the workplace. Non-millennials see themselves as above it all. *"Millennials are the problem and they should obey my golden rule: I have the gold; I make the rules—if you want my gold you need to follow my rules."*

I agree with that . . . to a point.

I am not about redistribution of wealth or egalitarian management systems, and I don't want to change who anyone is. I just want us to create an impact and rethink and change the way we work and the rules of the workplace for *everyone*. I want us all to be the best versions of ourselves, understand what that means, and leverage that to create better workplaces and results, both short and long term.

I'm not saying millennials aren't complicit in widening this gap. Of course they are, but let's be honest: What happens to us is principally because of us—*all* of us. If we want to get the best from our people, if we are to bridge this gap to create powerful relationships that take advantage of all of our strengths, we must accept that things have changed but we have not.

So how do we do all that?

We work from the inside out.

Empowering everyone starts with everyone—including you— working from the inside, starting with the one relationship you have that you can completely control: your relationship with *you*.

None of what we are doing to bridge the gap in this book will work if we don't know who we are first. Understand and enable yourself and you can *really really really* serve others. Trust yourself to be vulnerable, to work on yourself, to relish who you are, and then to share that with the world, and you will create the kind of relationships that deliver value to others *and* get results.

> We must first know, understand, and manage how we are perceived in order to manage others.

Simply put, the more you know yourself—truly know and care about yourself—the more you'll be able to truly know, care about, and connect to the people around you and achieve the relationships you need and want. So it's time to move forward in working on you and those relationships from the inside out—from you and outward toward others. The good news is only five short steps are required to complete this work.

Understand the power of **RELATIONSHIPS**		how you connect
Know your **STRENGTHS**		who you are innately
Recognize your **SKILLS, PASSIONS,** and **VALUES**		what you know and think of yourself and what you bring to the world
Define your **PERSONAL BRANDSTAMP**		who you are and want to be and how you want to be perceived in the world
Develop and deliver your **STORY**		how you present yourself to the world

Once you successfully complete these steps, you can effectively communicate who you really are and articulate your value in order to connect with others on an authentic level to bridge the gap in Part Two.

Step 1: Understand the Power of Relationships

"What's the most important life/work skill?" When we ask people this question in our launchbox workshops, at our clients' workplaces, in our extended professional networks, and at keynote presentations, the number one answer by far is "communication," followed by listening, discipline, passion, and persistence. (My teenage son Matthew said "forgiveness," so I asked him what he had done wrong.)

I'll take all of that. But I want something deeper. I want more. Communication and all the other answers are important, but they are components of the number one launchbox life/work skill.

BUILDING RELATIONSHIPS

Why is that true? Because *everything* revolves around relationships. Ultimately everything—from money and knowledge to power and love—boils down to interacting with other people. We are all human beings and human beings need relationships to survive. It is easy to get information any time from your smartphone, but how are you connecting? Caring is built on connecting. We want to connect—connecting with other human beings creates results. Even the most famous loner in American history, Henry David Thoreau, didn't choose Walden Pond for its solitude; he chose it because it was less than ten miles from Boston and just a short walk to the next cabin to borrow a shovel.

> Whether it is about money, knowledge, power, or love, ultimately every opportunity boils down to interacting with people.

Which is why every study I have read—and not just of millennials— shows that positive relationships lead to positive mindset and intent and are essential in business. Morale, productivity, innovation, loyalty . . . positive relationships lift all of these things and much more. Which is why countless business books emphasize the importance of relationships and identify them as the most critical factor for business and leadership success. I mean, can you think of a book that says, "Relationships are overrated. Kick people to the curb"?

We *know* this. So why do we, to use a very technical term, "suck" at relationships, especially when it comes to our millennial workforce? Why do we disconnect and dismiss instead of finding ways to connect? Is it just that we are not listening? Maybe. Just as likely, we don't want to or won't do the real work to build those relationships. But we must.

Simply put, relationships are the foundation of *trust*. Which is exactly what doesn't exist in most workplaces, or in many other disparate groups of humans, for that matter.

If we don't trust our people, why should our people trust us? (If Thoreau's neighbor didn't trust him to return that shovel, he'd never lend it to him.) Only with genuine relationships can we reestablish and build the trust we need to create workplace cultures founded on a genuine shared commitment to success and push everyone to *want* to be their best. Because *you* want to be your best, too.

Think of this as a customer relations problem. Companies across all industries spend some portion of their revenue on customer acquisition and relations. So let me ask you this: What would happen if your company treated your biggest and most important customers—regardless of their ages—the way you treated millennials? Most likely the customers' experiences would head south pretty quickly, leaving the company scrambling to figure out how to keep those customers from going someplace else. Yet that's exactly what we are doing with millennials—the biggest, most important part of our workforce, and in the marketplace, now and in the future.

We have failed to heed what Richard Branson, founder of Virgin Group, said so astutely: "Clients do not come first, employees come first. If you take care of your employees, they will take care of the clients." Thus the best approach to solving our millennial problem starts the same way as any customer relations problem: Be aware that you have a problem and then reach out to your clients (i.e., millennials) to reestablish trust.

Millennials need all the help they can get from us in this regard. They may be wireless like a Sonos speaker system, and connected with every other device to the Internet of Things all the time, but most of them haven't a clue how to make connections that start relationships. This is clear from the countless bad handshakes I have gotten at launchbox. Millennials look at me like I'm crazy when I say that the handshake matters, but it does. If they can't take ownership of something as simple as a handshake, what are they going to do with the more complex interactions?

Building relationships between managers and millennials starts from the inside out.

Think about it. Relationships are the most important thing in life, but who is teaching us how to make great relationships? Not teachers in high school, college, or graduate programs; gone are the days when Rotary, Kiwanis, Masons, houses of worship, and apprenticeships taught some of what we needed. I see plenty of tweeted platitudes and rants on my Facebook feed, but no actual instruction.

Our problems with young people start *before* we even begin to connect with millennials; we are not teaching any of what we need and expect from our people at home, in the community, or at the office. So when are millennials supposed to learn to be great connectors, relationship developers, and thus employees? When and where are they supposed to figure out what the rules are and what obligations they owe to themselves and to us to succeed? They have to learn it somewhere. They should just get it because we got it? *Really?*

Here is what I think of how true that is: Kids today don't know how easy they have it. When I was young, I had to walk nine feet through dense shag carpet to change the channel on my black-and-white TV. We did it all ourselves, right? No mentors at all. Well, I'm calling you on that, because even if you *did* do it yourself, how is that relevant today? Just like all those vacationless years and long hours that earned you that pot of gold, is that really what you want for the future? Is that the excuse *again* for abdicating any responsibility for changing the paradigm to create trust, build relationships, and make things better for everyone?

Here's a story about how easy it is to shift your mindset in a small way to care more about the relationships you have—and how easy it is to do the exact opposite. A lawyer friend of mine told me that a summer associate at his law firm had told him she would be late to her first meeting because of her breakfast with the intern recruiting program. My friend, the associate's supervising partner, could not believe she was late.

"What an insult!" he ranted to me. *[In his day . . .]*

"She is a millennial, right? And ostensibly smart? Harvard, Stanford, Georgetown student?" I asked.

"Yes."

"Do you think she really wants this summer intern position to turn into a permanent job offer at the end of the summer?"

"Absolutely."

"Right, she wants and needs this job. She's got $100,000 worth of debt, at a minimum."

"She would be aghast and mortified if she thought she was doing something wrong."

"So you get this. You get that she wants to be the best employee she can be."

"Yes."

"And prior to this meeting, her only connection with the firm had been the recruiting committee she had to have breakfast with. They are the only authority figures there she knows?"

"Sure."

"Okay, so let me ask you this: Did you coach her when she got to that meeting or before it even happened? Did you tell her directly the rules of the game—what she should and shouldn't know—so she could at least understand right and wrong? Or did you just shake your head in disbelief when she walked in late? Now, which path is your duty to her?"

I paused. I already knew the answer. And so did he. And so do you.

Come on! Let's own this duty and teach our people. The simplest scenarios like these offer us a chance to capitalize on what we as parents call teachable moments. But try and remember that teachable moments are two-way streets—both sides must grow from the opportunity to learn.

That's what relationships are, too: two-way streets. Only by cleaning our side of the street and learning who we are can we push others to clean up theirs. This will come into play in big way in Part Two; here it is the basis for challenging ourselves to make better

> Building powerful relationships in the workplace requires that both sides show up every day with resilient mindsets focused on delivering value, personal empowerment and accountability, authenticity, and shared results.

choices and to build trust and better relationships. That's how we take the step to deliver value to people through coaching and mentoring.

Remember: No one is teaching any of us, let alone millennials, to have better relationships with other human beings. This is a human problem, not just a business one. As David Brooks wrote in a *New York Times* Op-Ed based on his book *The Road to Character*: "We all know that the eulogy virtues [the ones talked about at your funeral] are more important than the résumé ones [the skills you bring to the marketplace]. But our culture and our educational systems spend more time teaching the skills and strategies you need for career success than the qualities you need to radiate that sort of inner light. Many of us are clearer on how to build an external career than on how to build inner character."

I couldn't have said it better so I won't try, except to add that reclaiming this inner light and character is more important than ever in business today. The caring that results leads to health, thoughtfulness and balance, connection and collaboration—and happiness.

This last point is not a hypothesis. Just watch Robert Waldinger's TED talk, "What makes a good life? Lessons from the longest study on happiness" (*bit.ly/1PxtGLt*). Waldinger is a clinical professor of psychiatry at Harvard Medical School and the director of the Harvard Study of Adult Development, which may be the longest study of adult life ever done. For seventy-five years, starting in 1938, the Harvard study tracked the lives of 724 men (about a third of them Harvard sophomores and the other two-thirds twelve- to sixteen-year-olds from inner-city Boston). As the men aged, the study asked them deep questions about their professional and personal lives.

And what did Waldinger say was the clearest message from this seventy-five-year study? "Good relationships keep us happier and healthier. Period." Waldinger then laid out three lessons he learned about those relationships.

1. *Social connections are really good for us, and loneliness kills.* The higher the quality of your relationship and the more socially connected you are, the happier, longer, and healthier your life is.
2. *People who were the most satisfied in their relationships at age fifty were the healthiest at age eighty*—cholesterol be damned.
3. *Good relationships don't just protect our bodies, they protect our brains.* When you can count on someone else and they can count on you, your memory stays sharper. (Which is why I said at the beginning I would have your back.)

Interestingly, in his talk, Waldinger also cited a study about today's millennials and their life goals, in which 80 percent said they wanted to be rich and 50 percent wanted to be famous. Turns out, the young adults in 1938 said the same thing. Chances are most people at that age would. But according to Waldinger, those "who fared the best were the people who leaned in to relationships, with family, with friends, with community." Simply put, Waldinger says, "Good, close relationships are good for our health and well-being, this is wisdom that's as old as the hills. Why is this so hard to get and so easy to ignore? . . . Relationships are messy and they're complicated and the hard work of tending to family and friends, it's not sexy or glamorous. It's also lifelong. It never ends."

Exactly. So knowing this, what are you going to do to connect and create great relationships? Because it starts with *you working from the inside out.* Not our businesses—we'll get to those integrated steps soon. To make your relationships with millennials stronger, we need to make *you* stronger first.

Step 2:
Know Your Strengths

At launchbox, we tell all our clients: "In order to know how to build, sustain, and maintain great relationships, we must understand the strengths of ourselves and others and how to leverage them effectively. Focus on your *strengths*—not weaknesses!" But we are acutely aware that those are just words; they don't show people how to do it. Which is why time with our clients—individual and corporate—starts with individualized baseline assessments (launchbox.com/assessments).

The key word in that last statement is not "assessment" but "individualized." We know, based on findings from Gallup, that effective leaders must understand their strengths and others' in order to create teams that meet the needs of the individuals, the team, the company, and the marketplace. So we start our work with a personal strengths assessment.

Let's create real personal relevance by doing some hardcore strength training—no excuses! Take the time now to answer the following question: *What are your top five strengths?*

> Strength training is leadership training.

Having trouble? Long before I started launchbox, I used Gallup's groundbreaking Clifton Strengthsfinder (*http://bit.ly/19Ge3R2*). Based on decades of research and experience, Strengthsfinder is an inexpensive yet highly evolved tool for helping people discover their unique combination of strengths. I encourage you to try it.

My Strengthsfinder strengths have evolved over the past ten years. Currently they are

1. **Activator:** I make things happen by turning thoughts into action.
2. **Communication:** I find it easy to put thoughts into words and am a good conversationalist and presenter.
3. **Strategic:** I create alternate ways to succeed and find relevant patterns and issues in any scenario.
4. **Significance:** I want to be very important and recognized in the eyes of others as making a difference.
5. **Command:** I have presence and want to take control and make decisions.

If you can't do Strengthsfinder or any other of the assessments out there, such as DiSC Profile, Myers-Briggs Type Indicator (MBTI), or the Wealth Dynamics Profile Test, just dig deep inside and write down what you see as your top five strengths. List them, consider them, show them to others, and test them. Ask family, friends, colleagues, and associates you trust to list what they think are your top five strengths. Reconcile the lists and list them in order right now, so that you can refer to it as you read on.

MY STRENGTHS

1. _____
2. _____
3. _____
4. _____
5. _____

The reason we do strength assessments is to help you *kick ass* the right way. That's right: Kick. Ass. Not kick someone else's ass. You've been doing that metaphorically in the wrong way, on your own, for too long, with your millennials, which is why you are chasing relevance with them.

> Becoming an ass kicker and being able to kick ass are privileges, not rights.

I mean kick ass to find your own relevance and purpose in everything you do, by not only understanding your strengths but also making a commitment to lead from those strengths. That's how you deliver value to yourself and others in a way that makes a real, quantifiable difference to everyone you touch. We will draw upon that idea in Part Two when we teach you how to become the leader and manager you were meant to be by leveraging the strengths of others.

For now, you only need to ask yourself: *What can I do to leverage my strengths and kick more ass for my people, teams, company, partners, clients, customers—everyone I touch on a daily basis?*

TO KICK ASS, ASK YOURSELF

1. Where do I kick ass?
2. I could kick more ass if . . .
3. Where do I wish I kicked ass?

Getting comfortable with your strengths is as basic as it gets for both kicking ass and understanding and finding relevance, by not going against your true nature. It's like that quote that some attribute to Einstein but is actually just a self-help line from the 1970s: "Everybody is a genius. But if you judge a fish by its ability to climb a tree, it will live its whole life believing that it is stupid." I agree! Don't apologize for who you are because you can't be who you are not.

But you know what is even *more* stupid? Being a fish and thinking you can climb a tree. Maybe you are terrible at something because you are working from a point of weakness rather than strength.

And you know what is even *more* stupid and alarming than being a fish and thinking you can climb a tree? Not knowing whether you are a fish or something else. That's what you're doing by not knowing and using your strengths—a crucial step that combines with the next steps we outline to articulate your personal value.

Step 3: Recognize Your Skills, Passions & Values

Strengths + (Skills + Passions + Values) = Your Value to Others

(the value you and your company deliver to others)

How do you know if you are delivering value to your team and clients? I mean *really* delivering. Can you tell me right now? Or better yet, just tell me how you define "value." To answer that about yourself and your company, you need to understand that equation. The same goes for corporate value (the value your business delivers to others). So what are the skills, passions, and values that define you and your business?

Skills

A skill is something that we have that others would value or that gives value to others. As opposed to strengths (which are natural predispositions or attributes), a skill is something you have actually learned, developed, honed, and/or have experience in doing that provides a benefit. And skills are incredibly hard to articulate. Go ahead and try it. List your three biggest personal skills.

MY SKILLS

1. _____
2. _____
3. _____

When I ask people to do this, most of them write attributes like "I'm a people person." Besides being a trite and meaningless line, that is *not* a skill. A skill answers another's question about your value, which by human nature is: *What's in it for me?* (WIFM). That's what other people are thinking when they ask you about your skills. "I'm glad you're a people person, but what is that going to do for me, my family, my clients, my business, and the world?" So to articulate an attribute as a skill, you need to think beyond yourself and change WIFM in your mind to "What's in for them?" or WIFThem. You are not a people person: Your skill is that you connect with other human beings immediately, which leads to stronger teams and client relationships. That's a skill. It is something you have learned *and* made about others. *That's* WIFThem.

It's stunning how much work in our launchbox coaching and workshops goes into helping people understand and articulate their skills with WIFThem largely because we are not trained to think that way. Think about what your best attributes mean to others or can do for others to earn you a job offer, more responsibility, their business, and their attention, and make those attributes into skills with WIFThem.

> You must actually be other-directed for your skills to connect to others. Make "What's in it for me?" about *them*.

- Don't tell me you "care deeply." That's great but what does it do for me in the workplace? Oh, you give great customer service and anticipate people's needs? *That's* WIFThem!

- Don't just say, "I innovate." What does that mean to *me?* Wait, you brainstorm on projects, so together we can come up with options others don't see to create real and meaningful opportunities? Nice WIFThem!

- You're "punctual"? What? Punctuality is a requirement of employment, not a skill. Oh, do you mean, "I'm calm and reliable—I won't make you wait or stress, and I'll always be there to offer support and understanding." *That's* WI-your punctuality-FThem!

- You're able to ask thought-provoking questions in any situation. Your skill is asking thoughtful, engaging questions that make people understand you have an interest in them. You care about solving their problems and you know how to systematically approach those problems and use their input to help solve them. WIFThem!

- You can analyze a spreadsheet. *So?* But being able to process complex quantitative data and information to help leaders give thorough advice to a client or manager? That's a tweetable WIFThem in 140 characters or less.

Go back and review your skills list now. Did you write other-directed skills or self-centered attributes? If you wrote attributes, go back and "skillfully" WIFThem-ize those attributes into skills. Now follow the same steps to define and WIFThem-ize your organization's skills as a business. The formula is the same as it was for your personal skills, and you need to explain them the same way—clearly, consistently, and concisely—before you move on to the next section.

- "We exceed our clients' expectations" WIFThem-ized is "We provide our clients with valuable information, resources, and opportunities outside the scope of the defined work but that we know will help drive their business."

- "We are good at solving clients' problems" WIFThem-ized becomes "We are curious and ask tough, insightful questions that push our clients. We then utilize what we learn to help them drive results in their business and seize new opportunities."
- "We coach clients' to be their best selves" in WIFThem turns into "We help clients understand themselves and then grow that understanding to help them connect, deliver value, and build relationships with others."

In the end, WIFThem-izing your corporate skills also ensures that those skills not only are being communicated the right way to clarify what you offer customers and clients but are also authentically aligned with your personal skills to connect with others and get results for your business.

Passions

Passions are easier to articulate, though we have been conditioned to bury them in the office as if we must be dispassionate at and about work. *Trust me, what defines you at work defines you personally, and vice versa.* We see in our one-on-one coaching and workshops that people who feel dissatisfied, stuck, and/or disconnected with their organizations, positions, career paths, and life in general or the obstacles in their way are usually disconnected from what makes their hearts sing. The work you do must align with what personally drives you. Figuring out those passions as part of this inside-out process sets you free to see that and much more. Most of our clients experience clarity of their own personal disconnects when they understand how their passions are out of alignment with what they are doing and how they are living.

So what makes your heart sing? What makes you happy? What do you laugh at? What are you compelled to do and what or who compels you to act? What do you choose to do when you have time? What would you do if money didn't matter? Your family, community, love, fairness, animals . . . list them now and commit them to memory!

WRITE OUT YOUR PASSIONS

_____

_____

_____

_____

_____

_____

_____

_____

Values

Values are not what you value—like hard work, family, and security. Those are passions and skills you may value in others. Values are your real-deal-no-BS-what-you-are-made-of principles or standards of behavior. Here are mine.

- empowering others to make a difference
- learning and satisfying my curiosity
- creating value for others and enabling their growth
- making meaningful connections

It sounds so easy and obvious, right? So why can't so many of us do it? Because most of us have not been conditioned to express those real-deal-no-BS-what-you-are-made-of principles. We're taught to suppress them. We express our company's values as our own, instead of aligning what we value as individuals with the company.

I love so many of the hundreds of books I have read on business, but most of them sell similar messages: Listen and grow. Change is tough but embrace it or die. Real leaders serve. People who succeed care about other people. Make it about others, not you . . . We've heard it all before. This extends to the most cutting-edge companies. Maybe you heard about Google's Project Oxygen, a 2009 initiative to identify what the best Google managers do, in order to teach their techniques throughout the company. The Google team mined the company's performance reviews, employee surveys, and other material to gather more than 10,000 observations of its managers' behaviors. The team analyzed the data and came up with eight things great managers do and then ranked them in order of importance.

Great managers need to . . .
1. Be a good coach.
2. Empower your team and don't micromanage.
3. Be interested in team members' success and well-being.
4. Don't be a sissy; be productive and results-oriented.
5. Be a good communicator and listen to your team.
6. Help your employees with career development.
7. Have a clear vision and strategy for the team.
8. Have key technical skills so you can advise the team.

These are simple and even obvious things to do. They are also effective. Did you really think Google—which asks interview questions like "How much does the Empire State Building weigh?"—would waste its time drilling for data and implementing the findings if it didn't expect high-level results? As the *New York Times* reported, "Once Google had its list, the company started teaching it in training programs, as well as in coaching and performance review sessions with individual employees. It paid off quickly." In fact, it improved manager quality for 75 percent of its worst performing managers within months.

That said, Zappos may not have mined data, but it still created its ten Zappos Family Core Values to live by, which the company consistently uses to develop its culture, brand, and business strategies.

Zappos Family Core Values
1. Deliver WOW through service.
2. Embrace and drive change.
3. Create fun and a little weirdness.
4. Be adventurous, creative, and open-minded.
5. Pursue growth and learning.
6. Build open and honest relationships with communication.
7. Build a positive team and family spirit.
8. Do more with less.
9. Be passionate and determined.
10. Be humble.

Love that. But is it bad to want to say "duh" when you read this list? Not at all. I've been doing many of these things for most of my career as a manager. We'd all do well to follow any of these Google behaviors or Zappos values. But I don't want you to adopt theirs.

First of all, you cannot say, "I want to be treated like we are Google" just because you are a high-tech company if you and your company don't value what Google values, especially if you don't understand the discrepancy. That's like saying you want to be Bobby Flay but not learn to cook. That's a surefire way to make sure millennials run for the door when they see the emperor has no clothes.

But here is the other thing: I don't want you to be the best version of Google or Zappos. I want you and your company to be the best versions of you and your company.

Consider a client of ours at launchbox, a former marine who had gone into real estate

Know what you and your business stand for *first*. What are your values?

sales. As one of the few and the proud of that branch of the US armed forces, he had served our country well. This man embodied the spirit of the marine motto, *Semper Fidelis* ("always faithful or loyal")—and indeed there has never been a mutiny among US Marines. But my client was about to revolt against his real estate job because he was horrible at it.

All because he could not articulate what his values were. He was a marine—faithful to the corps, "Ooh Rah" and all that. He knew their values, but not *his* values, once he left the corps.

For my client, going through his strengths, skills, and passions led to an *aha* moment when it came to his values. He suddenly realized something that is true about many millennials: His values were what drew him to his jobs—first as a marine and then to real estate. He saw the sale of homes as something that helped people and kept them safe, just like the marines. He changed his thinking from selling homes to make money for himself to helping, protecting, and serving people by selling them a home. He thought, *I am here to serve others and I need to think about serving others and providing value to them instead of just being a salesperson.*

Doing that changed his perspective—he started to feel like himself doing his job. He started asking people how he could better serve them and help them find the home they wanted. He was especially effective with military people who saw themselves reflected in him. That opened up tremendous opportunity. He sold eleven homes within months of finishing our course.

Even a marine has to learn to get out of his own way sometimes. So get out of your way and tell me your values first. Then do the same for your company.

I remember the first time I really did this well. I had joined an automotive group straight from a tech start-up. It was super strange for me going from a business with a Silicon Valley pedigree to a low-tech auto business owned by an entrepreneur from Alabama. But when he told me he would teach me everything I needed to know, I thought, *Wow, this guy created a $200 million business and he is going to teach me everything I need to* *know.* That's a big part of what made that boss special. He was the guide; he taught me.

Once I was aboard, we—the other partner, our HR director, Mary and Moose (our dynamic duo of consultants), and I—implemented an entire "inside-out" program with our managers, employees, and ourselves to build a great culture. My partner (probably the best partner I ever had and best man I ever knew—funny how those things go hand in hand) and I were given free range to do what was right and necessary to develop our culture and define its values. We did a yearlong company-wide culture tour and focus groups to come up with the values of how we wanted to treat our customers and who we wanted to be:

A FAMILY THAT . . .

was **F**un

had **A**ttitude

Made people's days

showed **I**ntegrity

Listened

believed in qualit**Y**

Through these values and as a family, we engaged our employees in the process. As a result, we made a thirty-year-old company as progressive in its values as Google, Zappos, or any others like Southwest and Virgin Group, in the news for the values they live every day. By getting out of our own way and putting aside what we thought we were and knew about each other, we nearly tripled the business over the six years I was there, and grew from four to eighteen stores with thousands of employees.

That's the power these operating values have. Take the time to articulate yours now. It doesn't need to be as involved as what I did in my business, but it does need to involve looking at your personal values first and then using them to express your business' values. That's how you articulate your real-deal-no-BS-what-you-are-made-of principles and standards of behavior. That's also how you take the first steps toward finding and defining yourself by creating your "personal brand-stamp"—a simple but not easy passport to unlocking a clear and concise story that further articulates your value.

Step 4:
Define Your Personal Brandstamp

The act of branding livestock with a fire-heated iron to identify ownership dates back to the ancient Egyptians. In business, the concept of "personal brands" dates back to the late 1990s. At launchbox, our approach to branding is considerably less painful than being touched by a hot iron (although millennials are not averse to marking; nearly 40 percent of them sport tattoos) and a fresh take on the value of defining your personal brand.

We call this your "brandstamp."

Brandstamps are about who you want to be, how you want to be perceived in the world, and whether or not you deliver on your brand. To help our clients define, articulate, and own their personal brands at launchbox workshops, keynotes, or peer-to-peer networking groups, we create brandstamps through an exercise you can start right now.

EXERCISE

Part One: Find Your Brandstamp Words

Yep, simple as that: Find three words that define your personal value and how you want to be perceived by the world. You can pick any three words you want to but try and pick

- words that are aspirational—that you think you are and wish to be perceived as—such as smart, caring, honest, and thoughtful.
- words that, when you wake up in the morning and immediately think of, make you push yourself to be your best.
- words that if you lived by them every day, you would be the best version of yourself and who you are meant to be.

To help you along, here is the launchbox list of personal brand words to use as a guide.

INNOVATIVE   Creative   Motivate   **BOLD**

Inspiring   **Teacher**   DESIRE   giving

Purposeful   Helpful   Trusting   Practical

Logical   Curious   **Intellectual**   EDUCATOR

comical   RESPONSIBLE   MINDFUL   **Direct**

Decisive   Mentor   Artist   Manager

Coach   Bright   Developer   Speaker

Salesman   **Specific**   Flexible   **Disciplined**

patient   Compassionate   Quick

Perceptive   caring   inquisitive   **thinker**

EXTROVERT   **powerful**   loving   generous

Athletic   smart   fun   humorous

adventurous   leader   accepting

OPEN   Eager   Listener   Presenter

EXERCISE

Part Two: Field-Test Your Brandstamp Words

Now that you have your words, test how well they are aligned with views people you know have of you, because the value you think you offer must be in alignment with the value others perceive in you.

Before I started launchbox, I struggled with what it would look like. My coach, Lauren, had an idea to assemble a group of thirty friends, former employees and bosses, peers, workout buddies, and mentors to discuss who I was and help me start to determine how I could build something big. Before I went in to talk with this group, I chose my own three words. Once we were assembled, Lauren and our facilitator, Angela, had the group pick the words they thought represented my personal brandstamp. They had fun joking and whittling down hundreds of words to three: direct, giving, and motivational. (I admit to being relieved when "arrogant" and "annoying" finally left the table.) Wow. Not only were they generous words (I felt like I was at my own funeral), but they also aligned quite well with mine at the time: generous, bold, and inspirational. To me, that meant I was living my story, and my story reflected who I was to them.

Note: As launchbox has evolved, so has my personal brandstamp. Today my words are generous, bold, and empowering. That is the cool thing about your words: they can evolve and you can change them whenever you need to, as long as you own them and keep them aligned with how people see you. In fact, it was my dear friend, personal coach, and launchbox guru, Giles, who said to me: "You need to change your word from inspirational to empowering. You don't give inspiration to people, you empower them to move, act, or do something. When they are around you, they want to be better. That, my friend, is empowering." After a few minutes of self-effacing doubt, I agreed; I want to kick ass for you and every millennial and non-millennial out there and so "empower" is what I do and who I am.

Your turn to try. Once you have your words, see how they align with the way your people see you, and listen to their comments. Do this with at least three people. See what they think your three words should be, then share yours and see if you are in alignment. If the words are aligned, congratulations! Live them and let them evolve as you do. If they are not aligned, get at it. Find out and explore the inconsistencies— seek to understand why disconnect exists—and get the words aligned.

And once they are? Go brandstamp yourself to own your commitment to your brand and to articulating your value daily. Follow this link http://www.launchbox365.com/brandstamp to get your own personalized brandstamp that we include with our workshops and coaching (because branding is cruel and a permanent tattoo might just be too millennial for you).

With that brandstamp in place, you are ready for the next, last, and hardest step in working from the inside out: integrating these values with everything you have learned and done so far to deliver your story. *Because when people see you as you see yourself, you are succeeding in conveying your value.* This is an essential foundation for telling your story and any story—even a company's story, which gets told through its culture, people, and the way it presents itself and treats its customers.

Step 5:
Develop & Deliver Your Story

*The plumber, the roofer and the electrician sell us a cure.
They come to our house, fix the problem, and leave.
The consultant, the doctor (often) and the politician
sell us the narrative. They don't always change things,
but they give us a story, a way to think about what's
happening. Often, that story helps us fix our problems
on our own. The best parents, of course, are in the
story business. Teachers and bosses, too.*

—Seth Godin, best-selling author of *Purple Cow* and *Linchpin*

I couldn't agree more. Human history has long known the power of
storytelling, from cave drawings to hieroglyphics to the oral traditions of
Native Americans to the Bible to Shakespeare to *Charlotte's Web*. In business, it is no different. The most influential business books of all time are
story based: Machiavelli's *The Prince*, Ken Blanchard and Spencer Johnson's *The One-Minute Manager*, and my favorites, Dale Carnegie's *How to
Win Friends and Influence People* and Napoleon Hill's *Think and Grow Rich*.

But I'll go Seth one step further: I believe *everyone* must be in the "story business" for us to be our best. It doesn't matter what business you are in or how charming you are: This is what's holding you back. If you want millennials to understand this, however, you'll need to show most of them what a gift being in the story business can be, and make owning your story the ultimate step in working from the inside out—a new kind of calling card in finding relevance.

We know the world is different from when previous generations started in business, and it continues to change. Just look at the market "Disruption Index" that follows. Consider all the stories about companies like Kodak, Blackberry, Sears, and Compaq failing to pivot before they lost relevance and died. Consider the new sharing and freelance economies created by Uber and Airbnb. Consider the world of social media and technologies that have changed the way we do business forever but that non-millennials never had growing up.

Once again we get that things are different. But understanding *why* it is different is critical to creating value in the workplace or marketplace.

Millennials have evolved faster technologically than any previous generation—and yet they are much less evolved when it comes to the

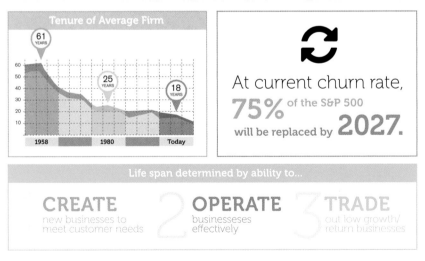

business of their stories. Technology has made the expectation of speed incredibly disruptive for all of us. We have gained a lot, but what have we lost? Why do we all lament the days of old like Angry John at the start of Part One? Because we have lost relationships—the connections that make us relevant as individuals to any generation.

We have lost the friggin' stories.

We have lost the one-on-one interactions and the deep bonds that come with them, which have tied us together since the beginning of time and have defined the intersection of history, family, business, youth, and experience. This is why we are drawn to them and feel compelled to watch them—even binge on them on Netflix. But no matter how many times we watch "Orange Is the New Black," we can't make up for the fact that we have lost the art and ability to connect by telling our *own* stories. Yet unlike non-millennials, who have forgotten the art and power of storytelling, millennials didn't lose their stories and the ability to deliver them; *they never fully developed them in the first place.*

That's what happened with my former-marine client in the real estate business. He didn't just need to articulate his values, he needed to communicate them through a story that made others understand them. He struggled mightily to do this. Once he did—working tirelessly to relate his work to his career as a marine and to his desire to pay forward how hard his single mother worked to give him a home and keep him safe— every person and group he presented to connected and wanted to work with him.

Given this marine's story was rooted deeply in who he was, why was it so hard for him to tell it? Because he had not been taught to value stories, nor seen their value modeled by the people around him. Because we as parents have been in the cure business, not the story business.

> We need to be in the story business instead of the cure business.

Millennials have lived a life controlled by hands-on parenting, protection from rejection, and stroked confidence (such as with massive grade inflation). They had endless choices but little free will as their parents hovered—watching, picking, lobbying for the best treatment, resolving problems, and soothing any pain. In fact, their parents' helicoptering seemingly knows no end. It started with teachers and coaches, then moved to professors. And now bosses bear the brunt: Forty percent of the HR and hiring managers in my professional network report being called or emailed by parents of their millennial employees because they complained to their parents, or the parents didn't like what their millennial kids told them about how they were being treated.

Really? *Yes, really.* This isn't a problem. It is an epidemic that has still-emerging consequences.

Then there are the parents who join their millennial children for interviews, or wait for them and ask to be introduced when it is over. Shocking—but it happens. These parents just have no idea how to close their book and enable *their* children to tell their own stories.

I never experienced a better example of this than when I met a mother and daughter working out with Ann, one of the coaches at our wellness center. The mother was a regular and her daughter, who was graduating from college, came along during spring break. When the mother found out that one of the other professionals in the workout group was in marketing, a career her daughter was eyeing, what do you think Mom did? Teach her daughter how to take accountability for herself and her goals?

No.

I watched as the mother took down the info of the person who could help her daughter *while her daughter just stood there.* I could not control myself and miss this coaching moment and I felt myself going . . . here I go . . . I can teach everyone . . . I can save the world from themselves or at least their helicopter parents. My mouth opened and out it spilled.

"Uh, hello, what are you doing?" I asked the daughter.

"What do you mean?"

"Where is your phone? Get it out. This is for you, not your mommy. I am betting your mom has had her first job already and knows how to do this. This is about *you* learning some real skills on how to get a job. Yes, it's *your* job to get your job. Get your phone. Go to notes. Dictate. Text. Take down the information and figure it out! This is your responsibility to learn how to do this for you, for your future, for your employer, and your future children."

They both stared at me blankly for a moment. Then Mom turned away and continued what she was doing.

I looked at Ann and she gave me that look. She knew how unbelievably unfulfilled moments like this make me—borderline incredulous and more than a little angry. Angry for all those kids who need to learn and don't have the opportunity to do so by telling their stories themselves because we cured; for all the kids who would be proud and eager to learn how to connect—if we let them. Those are the millennials who so want to add value but often can't, just as I couldn't here. I had to back down. The verdict against Mom was clear: guilty of cure, not teaching by story. This mother prevented her daughter from telling her own story to get a job.

This is what millions of moms and dads helicoptering throughout their kids' lives have wrought: blocking the ability of daughters and sons to have, let alone tell, their own stories and create real-deal relationships. They may have taught them to question everything. They may have told them how great they were. But they did not teach them this essential tool that they need to survive. The kids weren't told, allowed, or taught to tell their stories. The stories equal connection, which equal relationships—which equal better people and workplaces.

I crawled back to the launchbox offices and thought about my interaction the rest of the day. It gnawed at my perennial millennial soul. *How do I help people who are clueless that they are even in their own way?* How is that mother teaching her daughter to be an adult? Why is it *Mom's* job to get the email? Why does the daughter not care enough to stop her? Does the daughter even know how?

Then I remembered this mom wasn't even the exception that week. A mom had called me a few days earlier wanting help for her twenty-eight-year-old son. I told her to have her son call me and gave her my mobile phone number. She then proceeded to try and tell me about him and how he is different, and I said, "No, you don't need to tell me anything. If he wants to call me, I will help him. I don't need to hear anything from you. I just need to hear from him. That he wants help and he is interested in our services."

"Well, you don't understand. He—" After ten minutes of back-and-forth I told her I didn't think we were right for them because I didn't think she got what I was saying about having to hear his story *from him*. I told her, "I gave you my mobile number and said if your son needs help, have him call me directly, and I will give him an hour of my time for free to discuss and help him." But that wasn't good enough. She wanted to tell me what his problem was and how to solve it. Tell me again why we are surprised when millennials show up in our offices with limited senses of who they are and how to sell themselves?

> You need to understand your own strengths and deliver your own story to be able to connect with and provide value to others.

It is incredibly ironic that we have created a world that has gradually devalued or eliminated our ability to tell stories, considering that the current trend in retail and customer service—and what resonates with millennials—is all about stories. We increasingly look for them to understand, rationalize, and feel good about the products we buy and the food we eat. Companies advertise these stories to get us to buy in to what they are selling. The origins of our coffee or chocolate, who grew the vegetables on our plates and raised the animals we eat, who designed and where and how those jeans and shirts were made, who created that line on Etsy, who milked that goat for this soap . . . The more authentic the stories are, the more we connect and stay loyal.

We crave stories that affirm the value of our purchases, yet suck at offering them when it comes to valuing *us*. As a nation, we need to get back to storytelling about us, owning and sharing our stories to create deep and genuine relationships that bind and fulfill us. We need to get back to the days of Rotary Clubs, Kiwanis, houses of worship, mentorship, apprenticeship, and teaching. *We need to enable everyone to tell stories.*

To do this, Mommy and Daddy need to do the same thing we need to do as leaders in general and as leaders of their children in the workplace: enable millennials to really communicate and connect with people. But it is hard to connect with others when you don't know, and can't tell, your own story. If you are in a management relationship and you are trying to create real trust with your millennial employees, you need to help them discover and articulate their own stories—maybe for the first time.

So use your strengths and your skills, passions, values, and brand-stamp to develop and deliver your story, define your relevance, and connect with others and the world.

This is the ultimate step in working from the inside out—it is the behavior we most need to lead the changes we need to succeed. Learn to help your children, millennials, employees, and everyone you connect with by teaching them how to share and articulate their stories. We all have great qualities. Let's share them and play them up to make meaningful connections. That's the secret to success in building the relationships we need: connecting with each other by sharing ourselves through clear and concise communication and articulation of value through great stories.

Stories build connection with your employees and customers. Unlike the usual static, boring, impersonal presentations and platitudes, stories resonate with others. They have drama and arcs. By delivering your story well

- you build that elusive trust with others that makes you credible and gets them to "lean in."
- you connect and create common ground with your employees on a deeper emotional level.

- you communicate value, defining and giving meaning to the journey you (and thus your people) are on.
- you show wisdom and humility.
- you persuade and inspire action.

Much of this is often true even for stories that happened to others but are told by us. The key is to use all you have to make the stories you tell resonate: emotions, drama, humor, irony, self-deprecation. Nancy Duarte's *Resonate* offers more help with these tools for bigger and more formal presentations, but I find that the tools serve you well in what I call "drive-by's"—quick, momentary opportunities to seal the deal.

I think I tell at least fifty stories a day, using each one to make a point as it relates to my audience at the time. Whether in a meeting, on a client call, at a cocktail party, at the gym, on the sidelines of a lacrosse field, in a coaching session, at a keynote during a Q&A, or just when I say good morning to someone on the street, I am always sharing and connecting through stories. Is it exhausting? Yes, but it's empowering for the people I engage with and for me—and an amazing tool for starting great relationships at every turn, helping me find that happiness Robert Waldinger spoke about in his TED talk.

Of course, not every story is for every situation—including my own, as you will see in a moment. So here are some tips about what I do to tell the right stories, whether to a party of one or 1,000, to give you some connection juice.

- When choosing your story, first take the temperature of the room, where you are, and who your audience is.
- Ask yourself: *What does my audience need? Who are they? What can I do to get closer by sharing something in common or at that moment that will get my audience to lean in?* Can you share situational awareness, information about customers, projects, a

restated goal, something meaningful about what your boss told you about how proud of the team he was? Have you been there before and can you explain what happened that time?

- What is special about you and them together at that moment? Do you have something that connects to what your audience needs to hear to get results and win?

The key is to use all you've got to make sure it is fresh and real. Anything can work: what's going on in the news; what you are dealing with personally; how you started your day; what fear you overcame just recently; a funny thing that happened with your kid, boss, employee, or spouse and how it is relevant to connecting to and helping your audience.

A general rule? Kids and puppies always work great. Sports and pop culture, too. Shoot for humorous but not jokey stories and make sure they are real. For example, as I alluded to earlier, my teenage son Matt had bonked a big test (sorry, Matt). This was part of his ongoing problems with homework and tests, and I was pissed off beyond belief. I told him "the party was %$#@! over!" That I owned him now, and rules would be put in place to deal with this once and for all.

Matt responded with typical witty bewilderment but seemed to understand things were a little different. And you know what? Damned if he didn't start to turn his grades around. After making him go and ask for feedback, his mother and I got really positive descriptions of his efforts and successes from his teachers, and the tone of our conversations started to change. After a period of sustained success, Matt asked for more privileges back. I called him to discuss that, and to congratulate him—to tell him that I was so proud of him. But I also told him that now I knew how smart he really was and could be, it was game on for him. He needed to continue to perform well in school.

That's when Matt asked me, "Dad, is this a good call or a bad call?

"What do you think?"

"I am not sure. That's why I'm asking."

"Well, you turned around your grades, you are capable and smart, and your dad is now going to help make sure that you are successful. Is that good or bad? You get to choose."

"I'm gonna go with a good call."

My son is infinitely wise . . .

And there you have it: A story about choice that could be applied to how to interpret news and situations as good or bad, or choosing your mindset and understanding situations at work as positive or negative (something that will help you greatly in Part Two). How can you bring those things that happen to you in life and share them through storytelling to create connected relationships? The better you become at it, the more ready you will be to go deep and tell your own story.

Let's be honest: The main reason people won't or don't go deeper is not because they reject stories on principle or don't believe stories are effective, but for the same reason people don't like change. Like change, storytelling is difficult and sometimes even uncomfortable. It is not what we've been taught to do, and it is hard—just like relationships. And here is the truth about the secret of why change is hard: We all probably really suck at telling our stories. Actually, it is appalling how bad people are at telling their story, let alone connecting it to what they do. I sucked too for the same reason you do: We do not focus enough on storytelling from elementary school to high school to college to graduate school to the workplace. As a result we can't even tell our stories to ourselves in the mirror, let alone one-on-one or god forbid to a group or audience. After all, fear of public speaking ranks higher than death in most surveys. So we can't tell our stories and fear telling them more than death . . . how the heck are we going to connect?

> Building and maintaining relationships requires us to tell our stories.

This is why at launchbox, we constantly work on stories with millennials and managers at keynotes, workshops, through coaching, and in our software platform. It is the most critical element. We do it with all types: millennials, managers, parents, kids, and clients who come from every industry, be it retail, high-tech, biotech, law, accounting, the military, and beyond. The full launchbox process requires a level of interactivity and intimacy that is beyond a book, but let's do some "Speedcoaching" around storytelling with three simple questions asked and answered quickly.

- **Who am I?** Where was I born? Where do I come from? Who is my family? What is my background—my family identity? What am I grateful for? What and who have made me who I am?
- **What is my experience?** What work have I done? What am I inspired and motivated by? What am I passionate for and about? What have I had to overcome, and what are my triumphs?
- **What value do I bring?** What am I good at? What are my special skills? What has made me unique and special? Why do people love me, and what do I do to maintain that? What kind of attitude do I have? What can I do for others? What about me makes me successful that is not about my technical experience?

Go ahead and answer these questions. Once you have the answers, look for connections to your strengths, skills, passions, values, and personal brandstamp. The earlier steps have been setting you up for this: to craft a story that unites your strengths, skills, passions, values, and personal brand words; allows you to share them; shows how you live them; connects them to what you do; and makes you own who you are, to forge genuine connections with others that lead to results.

Even without the work in Part Two, there are simple ways to channel the energy of the story you create and deploy it to bridge the gap with your people.

- Use yourself as an example when talking with the team.
- Tell a story that creates common ground about the work at hand.
- When team members are struggling, invest in them. Find a story to share, authentically using their strengths, skills, passions, values, and brandstamps as a foundation to launch them so they get better.

Remember, your story is not a script. You don't get penalized for not telling it exactly the same way each time. It is merely a framework to understand yourself in a visceral way and an outline for interacting with people. It is connection currency you can take to the bank. And you'll rarely, if ever, get to tell it all at once. Telling it all at once is what I call puking on someone (except with words) for three minutes straight. Ouch! *Please* don't do that. You need to be able to put your whole story together and then take it apart, building it up like blocks, in sections, depending on what the situation calls for and what the people you are trying to connect with need. Think of it as your roadmap to connecting.

I can break out my story, which has evolved over time (my current model as I write this book follows), to answer any question, trigger related stories that might help in any given situation, and connect with any human being. Peppered in the story is who I am, where I am from, what value I bring to others, and my strengths, skills, passions, values, and personal brandstamp in a form that provides value to others. I need only to be the master of my story to adapt it to what I need to do—pitch a client, connect with a potential employee, make a friend, start a conversation at a gym or on a plane, talk to my children or their friends . . . it works anywhere with anyone.

My Story

People have always told me "no." I hate that no. It just compels me to push harder. As a kid, that no sometimes meant I got told I was just a difficult child, or I got the shit kicked out of me. As an adult in business, it's made me a maximizer, because the reason behind the hate has always been the same: I want people and situations to be better than anyone imagines they could be—I want to empower people, help them, push them to be their best. I want to right what is wrong, make things just, and confirm that people understand exactly how things are going down to ensure that real value is exchanged. The sheer joy of being able to unstick others and launch them through coaching, training, speaking, managing, and assessing the gaps between them and what they want and need to do has been nothing short of mind-blowing. It is my drug.

But there is a pain at my core that fuels my zeal to solve problems for others and shapes my advocacy for what I feel should always be present in life—love of self, safety, clarity, empowerment, and growth. I grew up in a broken and abusive household. My father moved out and I got a new layer, a monster of a stepfather who made sure violence and alcohol were always present. To combat it, I developed a no-nonsense brand of brazen attitude, quick wit, sharp tongue, and fierce protectiveness—and a desire to help others. But it took some time for me to completely understand how to do this professionally and make what I do work for everyone, including me.

That understanding started with my mentors. I became a personal and professional seeker of people who could help me build wealth and prove my worth in this world. To get out of my broken home, initially I was drawn to close-knit families who could model what I eventually wanted for *me*. I was, and continue to be, especially attracted to survivors—I survived my home life and later also survived cancer. I spent a lot of time with my friends' families, including one whose patriarch was liberated from a Nazi concentration camp, immigrated to the United States, and became a multimillionaire. His brand of storytelling, thoughtfulness about what was right, and perseverance led me to understand the importance of education. I had always been street smart and insatiably curious, but this man's success, and the purity and simplicity of his entrepreneurial wisdom, propelled me to the next level of how to relate with people. Members of another family became my first business partners and demonstrated the value of grit and hard work in being a merchant, and the value of selling.

These mentors, my mom, and my biological dad taught me that education would be the path to make it happen. They were more right than they even knew, because in college I met my wife. She singlehandedly exposed me to a new reality, or you might say reality in general. Together, we created the thing I wanted most in life: a real family—*my* family. And what an amazingly cool family it is. Three kids (fun and cool millennials, two mostly launched) and a village of people: friends, business partners, coaches, advisors, workout buddies, and clients. After having such poor examples growing up, they are my inspiration and my rock, and they're all critical to my success.

But to understand that was a continual work in progress. After college, my wife and I both entered law school, where I learned how to sell, provoke, speak, ask questions, create relationships, and deliver value. I then used those skills to acquire new experience and mentors outside the law. Everywhere I went, I sought someone to "take me in," and teach me something new about what I wanted to be and who I was. From hotdog carts to restaurants to companies that sell cars, build technology, or serve clients, I met entrepreneurs and zealous artists that I fell in love with immediately. Along the way there were great successes (private jets, fast cars, houses, first-class trips) and many failures (being fired on more than one occasion, economic uncertainty, mistakes, broken trust, lousy business partners). As a result, I had both a big ego and a chilling lack of confidence.

It wasn't until my forties that I finally understood that for all the wonderful mentors I had, I was missing an essential one: myself. I needed to seek the mentor within me and share him with myself. I survived my childhood. I beat back cancer and today I eat right, exercise, and practice mindfulness to keep that cancer at bay and my head straight. I had all the business and personal successes I would ever need. But only when I found *me* did everything feel right. Whether managing a team of thousands, growing sales by the tens of millions, creating workplace cultures, giving legal advice, or mentoring friends, family, or colleagues, I now use the power of connecting with my story not to make it about me but to be other-directed.

Yes, it happened from the inside out—and that led to even more influence. I no longer chase relevance; I create it for myself and help create it for others. Owning that internal relevance is especially critical to being relevant to next-generation leaders. How can I help you launch yourself, your team, and your company to be better, kick some business ass, and bridge any and all gaps you face?

Now it's your turn. Write your story and learn to deliver it. Then repeat the same process for your business' story. Learn how to articulate your value to others in that format. So many people are hesitant to tell their story because they think it's self-promotion or bragging. Heck no. The secret sauce of your story is exactly the opposite: It's about putting yourself out there to help others by establishing your relevance. That's what makes Oprah, Bill Clinton, Richard Branson, Sheryl Sandberg, Bruce Springsteen, and other great storytellers so successful—they can tell their stories and listen to and then tell the stories of others, to make you feel genuinely connected. That's what makes companies like Google, Starbucks, Nike, Apple, Disney, Zappos, Tesla, Levi's, and other brands that tell and sell great stories so powerful. They know who they are and communicate that to the world. Know, however, once you complete this task, you are still only Part One of the way there.

MAKE IT HAPPEN:
Work from the Inside Out

Now that you've successfully completed these five steps, you can effectively communicate who you really are and articulate your value to connect with others on an authentic level. In Part Two, you'll take your story and apply all the inside-out work you have done so far as a foundation to build relationships with your team. You'll empower your team to do the same to deliver value and results to you as a leader, and to themselves, the company, and your customers. Because the more you know yourself—truly know and care about yourself—the more you'll be able to truly know, care about, and connect to the people around you to achieve the relationships you need and want.

Just remember the five steps of Part One, as you'll need them along the way.

1. **Connect through the power of relationships.** Whether it is about money, knowledge, power, or love, ultimately every opportunity boils down to interacting with *people*.

2. **Know and leverage your strengths.** Strength training is leadership training.

3. **Recognize your skills, passions, and values.** Strengths + (Skills + Passions + Values) = Personal Value, the value you deliver to others—remember to turn "What's in it for me?" (WIFM) into "What's in it for *them*? (WIFThem).

4. **Define your personal brandstamp.** Know who you want to be, how you want to be perceived in the world, and whether or not you deliver on that.

5. **Develop and deliver your story.** Building and maintaining relationships requires us to tell our stories to the world. Use your stories to share who you are, your experiences, and how you can add value to others.

PART TWO

B.R.I.D.G.E. the Gap

*People don't care how much you know
until they know how much you care.*
—John Maxwell, *Winning with People*

What Is B.R.I.D.G.E.?

B.R.I.D.G.E. is an overlapping and integrated six-step plan that unleashes the power of your inside-out work. It compels you to understand your own relevance to address disconnects and become completely relevant as a guide, mentor, and leader with and to millennials. B.R.I.D.G.E. does this first and foremost by building genuine and caring relationships that increase engagement, productivity, innovation, results, and profits to empower you and your people to connect, mentor, lead, motivate, and add value at the highest levels. Do the hard work that each part requires and you'll have the right tools and skills to be a better manager and to develop your millennial employees for the benefit of the company. You'll also have a more connected, productive, fun, enjoyable, and significant professional and home life.

That's a mouthful, huh? Try thinking of it this way then: B.R.I.D.G.E. is like a recipe and a cooking lesson combined. It takes the inside-out ingredients from Part One and turns them into a delicious dish to serve to others. To become and remain other-directed, you need to

- **Bust myths** to identify and break through underlying assumptions about employees that create barriers.
- create **Real-deal**, authentic, caring relationships with your team.
- develop an **I own it** mindset that forces you to be personally accountable and responsible for driving results.

- **Deliver value** through understanding, mentorship, and coaching of others.
- have meaningful and aligned **Goals in mind** based on a shared and embraced vision.
- **Empower success** through leveraging strengths, paving the road to success, and giving feedback and recognition the right way.

Don't be fooled by the apparent simplicity of it all. This is easy to say but hard to do. Or as my boss in the auto business told me, "Dan, it's all simple; it just ain't easy." To get started in the right direction, all I ask of you now is what my bosses in that auto business asked me to do: *show up*. Show up and do what needs to be done on your end to B.R.I.D.G.E. the gap with your people and write new rules for the workplace of the future. Yes, you—*you* need to show up. B.R.I.D.G.E. the gap and show how much you care.

B: Bust Myths

Identify and breakthrough underlying myths and assumptions about employees that create barriers.

#AssumePositiveIntent

Let's start by taking a little quiz. Do the following statements about millennials ring mostly true or mostly false?

- They have a sense of entitlement, and expect everything now!
- They're lazy and don't want to work hard like we did; work/ life balance is more important than hard work.
- They are disloyal and jump ship if they are not engaged or growing.
- They need feedback all the time, 24/7/365. ("Please tell me how great I am. Every day. Twice.")
- They have different career goals from non-millennials.
- They want everything digital.
- They don't deal well with authority.

Here's the answer: It was a trick question.

All these are true . . . and false . . . and none of that matters. They are *assumptions*—myths, really—and there is no right or wrong when it comes to them. That's because while myths, assumptions, stereotypes—whatever you want to call them—may be false as blanket statements ("all Americans are overweight" and "all fashion models are anorexic"), they come from a place of partial truth (more than two-thirds of Americans *are* overweight and many models *are* unrealistically thin). But who wants to be viewed through the lens of myths like these?

> What are the myths or assumptions that you have about millennials? What are the myths or assumptions they have about you?

Consider the quiz from the other side. Do the following statements about non-millennial managers ring mostly true or mostly false?

- They obey the Golden Rule: "I've got the gold, I make the rules!"
- They are only in it for the money.
- They are inflexible and don't like change; they're stuck in their ways.
- They are *so* not tech savvy.
- They don't care about their teams or people.
- They are "hard graders" and couldn't care less about recognizing others.
- They are afraid of nontraditional approaches.
- They are willing to trade the pursuit of true passion for stability.

If you are a non-millennial manager, does this sound like you? Or sound like how you want to be perceived in this world? Well, these are the things most millennials say about us. How much is true? Not much, right—they are myths. And just as you are guilty of creating myths that lead to disconnect and frustrations with millennials, they are guilty of perpetuating myths about you. How does either lead to better connections and relationships?

To get away from these assumptions and bust myths on both sides, we need to

✓ "Breakthrough" generational stereotypes.
✓ Understand and value different work styles.
✓ Focus on and assume positive intent.

Breakthrough Generational Stereotypes

The use of the word "breakthrough" is intentional. "Busting myths" does not just mean stopping the nonsense to identify and break through underlying assumptions and barriers to figure out the real people you have and what they're made of. Busting myths means a real breakthrough in understanding, connecting, and caring for all of us non-millennials who must lead and define expectations for *everyone*. But we can't do this by assuming we know it all, are doing everything right, and are minimizing the frustrations and disconnects that millennials feel in the workplace.

Think back to the introduction and the graphics that listed disconnects between millennials and their managers: lack of trust, not encouraged to participate in important decisions or share ideas, not listened to, lack of feedback and guidance on performance, no resolution of issues and handling of conflict in a positive manner, not showing any interest in personal well-being . . . The point isn't whether managers agree or disagree with these disconnects; the point is managers assumed they did many of these things well, such as establishing trust, encouraging participation, and giving feedback and guidance.

That's the word that's causing us problems: "assume." *We must identify and break through underlying assumptions, stereotypes, and barriers about millennials that are impacting our relationships with them.*

Truth is, just as Socrates complained about young people like Plato, young people have always railed back with their own blanket statements about their elders. (Imagine Plato with a pierced eyebrow and neck tattoo.) As a Gen Xer, I remember what boomers thought of my generation: a bunch of whiny slackers sure to accelerate the world's decline. They thought Gen Xers didn't care and weren't willing to pay their dues—just what most non-millennials think about Gen Y or millennials. But what did we do? We resisted. We pushed back for some family time, refused to suffer in suits or high heels all day, encouraged creativity in the workplace, and embraced new technologies. We rolled with the punches of multiple recessions and economic shrinkage—or at least we tried to.

So tell me again why we want millennials to face similar struggles?

"But my millennials are so *annoying*." Got it. Remember, millennials look nothing like the previous generations, and that's why they annoy you. It's a lack of understanding of and between different generations and an unwillingness to flex to other generations' needs and working styles.

The point is, millennials are probably everything and nothing we say about them. You can find any fact you want to support any myth you want to perpetuate. No less a trusted source than *The Economist* noted that every piece of evidence about millennials could be contradicted by another piece of evidence. Almost daily, it seems. Hundreds of news stories about millennials fill my inbox every week, many of them featuring a new study by a reputable organization that contradicts another recent study by another reputable organization. According to the U.S. Chamber of Commerce Foundation's *Millennial Generation Research Review*: "Millennials are likely the most studied generation to date. . . . There are data to find pretty much whatever you are looking for, as the data are varied and sometimes contradictory. In fact, Millennials are full of contradictions, which, of course, may explain the youth of any generation."

- Entitled, lazy, and won't do what they're told? In a poll of 5,000 workers by Jennifer Deal of the Center for Creative Leadership and Alec Levenson of the University of Southern California, 41 percent of millennials agreed that "employees should do what their manager tells them, even when they can't see the reason for it," compared with 30 percent of baby boomers and 30 percent of Gen Xers.

- Millennials aren't competitive? *The Economist* cites research by CEB, a consulting firm that polls 90,000 American employees each quarter, that 59 percent of millennials say competition is what gets them up in the morning much more than the percentage of baby boomers or Gen Xers that say that about competition.

- They only communicate digitally? That study by Jennifer Deal and Alec Levenson showed that more than 90 percent of millennials surveyed want face-to-face feedback and career discussions.

- They jump ship and are not committed for the long term, or really *any* term? According to the US Bureau of Labor Statistics, the average worker stays at a job 4.4 years, and yes, according to the Future Workplace "Multiple Generations @ Work" survey of 1,189 employees and 150 managers, 91 percent of millennials expect to stay less than three. But beware of averages: Millennials may be willing and find it normal to job-hop faster than any previous generation, but when they find the right opportunity they actually are *more* loyal than the previous generation. In fact, the CEB study showed millennials put future career opportunity among their top five reasons for choosing a job, again ahead of other generations.

Simply put, when it comes to millennials, most of us have no idea what to believe or do. So we believe and assume the worst.

Until we see this, the most powerful myths or assumptions that we have about millennials will continue to negatively impact our attitudes about, perceptions of, and relationships with them. This is no different from when you have relatives or friends whom you think of as selfish. They may have been selfish in the past, so when you see them, you always view them through that negative "selfish lens" (like rose-colored glasses, but in reverse). It overwhelms the positives and blinds you to them. Unless you become aware of the lens, remove it, and see those people without judging them, the negative perceptions and assumptions will dominate.

> Get past the myths and realize that individual differences are more important than generational ones.

A professor I know wanted to ban her millennial students' digital devices. They were all using them. She was sure they were all on the Internet and social media, or texting—completely disengaged from her class. Of course, some were using the devices to take notes, as they had probably done for most of their note-taking lives, but even with her best classes, she was getting annoyed—until she took off her selfish lens and asked the students what they were doing. Turns out, many of the students were using their devices to look up more information about what she was talking about. And it changed the way she engaged those millennials in class. They could look up facts and figures to support, debate, or understand what she was saying, while she used the time to engage them with ideas.

We can do the same in the workplace. For example, "Older people don't treat me with respect" is a common complaint from many millennials, while non-millennials say "Respect must be earned; you earn respect by following the rules and working hard to achieve success. These 'kids' have no work ethic." Really? Or do they just not have *your* work ethic? Better to change them to look like us, right? *No!* What does a tongue ring have to do with IQ? Is loyalty about how you work and act, or about effort and results? Is someone stupid or disloyal simply because they don't act the way you do—even if they give you everything they have?

Millennials need leaders (especially the cure kind), not parental figures. Treat them as stupid and they'll ignore or reject you. What would you do if it were you?

- **STOP** placing anyone in one box.

- **START** engaging millennials to take advantage of their strengths and see how they can complement yours.

Again, this goes back to the age-old challenge every generation faces. Socrates and generations before him and since have struggled to get past their assumptions to understand and value different work styles of other generations and their benefits. Those assumptions become the foundation of our frustrations with and disconnects from millennials, when in fact our values are not so far apart.

Understand and Value Different Work Needs, Values, and Styles

- What makes each generation/person tick?
- What does each generation/person need/prefer?
- How can you leverage the strengths of each?

Millennials' work needs and values are not all that different from those of their managers; they just see life more opportunistically and have a deep desire to be well-off financially as quickly as possible. As noted in the introduction, millennials grew up through the boom and bust at the start of the twenty-first century. As a result, they lack the optimism of previous generations. They've seen the layoffs. They know commitment is not a two-way street. Yet in the end, the work needs and values of millennials aren't so terribly hard to stomach even if they can't articulate them very well.

Now take off the millennial lens to understand the different work styles of each generation and accept that millennials and non-millennials have contrasting but not conflicting styles, beliefs, and expectations. They may be different, but they are in many cases complementary.

SUPERVISORS		MILLENNIALS
Command and control management style	MANAGEMENT STYLE	Active, involved leadership
Individually focused	WORK STYLE	Collaborative
Managed flow of information	INFORMATION INTAKE	Unstructured flow of information
Job security	EXTRINSIC MOTIVATION	Employability / capability
Work = income	VIEWPOINT	Work = income and personal enrichment
Structured	ENVIRONMENT	Flexible
Inward looking	PERSPECTIVE	Outward looking
Through organization, position	INFLUENCE	Through networks, communities
Standard performance reviews, hard to deliver	FEEDBACK	Want it 24/7/365, hard to take
Need to know basis	INFORMATION ACCESS	Transparency
Infrequent	CELEBRATE	Critical

In the end, most millennials just want what we all want. They also want bosses who care, set clear expectations, and are willing to coach—and who understand what they expect and need in the workplace.

Are these things so unappealing or are they just not your story? Don't let difference breed contempt.

- 💬 Collaboration
- ⭐ Work-life balance
- 🔍 Transparency
- ✅ Authenticity

- 🧩 Challenge
- 📝 Flexibility
- 📌 Purpose
- ⚙️ Engagement

Take flexibility. Is it all that hard to check in with your people and provide flexible work schedules to accommodate the fitness, family, and fun millennials seek in their "me" time? Millennials believe deeply in individuation. They want to get better and feel better, and integrate mind, body, and career. According to Jean M. Twenge, professor of psychology at San Diego State University and author of the recently revised *Generation Me*, "Work/life balance is an important factor in millennials' employment decisions.

> Is the important thing how someone does something or the results they get doing it?

Perhaps the cultural shift toward individualism and positive self-views has promoted the idea that we're entitled to a little 'me' time."

Think about what Twenge says through the lens of this millennial.

> I want things to have meaning so I search for it constantly. The previous generation thinks we are lazy and we don't want to do the work like they did. And that is true. We don't want to do it your way. But we *do* want to work. I just don't want to compromise who I am.

Or consider collaboration. Creating opportunities for millennials to connect, collaborate, and network with colleagues, customers, and the community leverages the collective genius of all stakeholders. But that goes for managers, too, who understand this on a deeper level than millennials ever have. No one wants to just work online and crowdsource every decision. Millennials may be conditioned to do this, but they want to connect on a deeper level, too. They feel okay about asking for input and help and working together. But they want the intimacy of a one-on-one connection and collaboration, too.

Think what this millennial said about her work with a name partner at her office: "One time, one of the partners spent two hours on the phone with me, going line by line through research I'd drafted. She offered constructive criticism and imparted her thoughts. She did not have to do that with me. It was the best day out of the entire year I had worked there. And I let her know how much I'd appreciated it."

That kind of collaboration should naturally lead to greater engagement. Engage and give feedback, feedback, and more feedback, and then ask for feedback in return to create the ultimate in self-accountability for productivity and profits—and do it without couching words or BS. Remember: Communication is *not* something millennials are very good at. You push, but meet resistance when you ask. Fair enough. Millennials must be responsible for asking for feedback and knowing the goals, but so must the manager. Stop whining about things; be open and honest to help them hone and develop their skills. If the work is subpar through no fault of yours, say, "Hey, you did a really crappy job on that assignment. Let me show you how to do it better." And *keep* doing that.

Not very complicated, but we have a challenge in doing it. That millennial who savored the collaboration with her boss over the work she did? She also told me: "Sadly, though, nothing else even close to that has happened since then."

Therein lies the rub. It takes hard work to change and then sustain that change over time. But when we do it, the immediate results will be engagement on an entirely new level. And we already know the importance of engagement from every management book ever written. Engaged employees take fewer sick days, perform better, cost less money, come up with better ideas . . . all great reasons to engage millennials on deeper levels and stop hiding behind assumptions.

Most of all, remember: Millennials want to feel capable. They need to learn and grow—they will endure a lot of pain if you can describe to them what they are learning and how they are growing. They may be restless to climb the ranks, but it is mostly about finding more value

Do you understand the importance of "capability" to millennials?

for their futures. How good are you at letting them know that is what they are getting—or that you are actually doing that for them? Have you created an environment of capability—learning and growing—for your *best* millennials, or at least enlisted them in helping create it? Or have you let your assumptions about all of them undermine your feelings and actions?

Assumptions about differences breed resentment; understanding differences breeds respect. What can you do tomorrow to breakthrough/ break through myths and start assuming positive intent?

Focus On and Assume Positive Intent (API)

Even with my wife, whom I love and trust more than anyone in the world after thirty-plus years together, I need to remember that she did not say something critical or biting to rip my heart out. Or when I am feeling critical, pouty, annoyed, negative, or just in a funk—which for all my inside-out work still happens often—I need to remind myself to be my best self and not say something I might regret later. This is especially true when it comes to dealing with people who have given me no direct reason to assume the worst other than being "not me."

As easy as this is to write, it all takes constant work and perseverance to do, and we all need help doing it in our personal, and especially, our professional lives. That's how a Mexican spiritual teacher, Don Miguel Ruiz, became a best-selling author in 1997 with his book *The Four Agreements: A Practical Guide to Personal Freedom*. I often resort to the agreements as a primer for shifting from negative assumptions to positive intent to create what Don Miguel calls a larger picture of unconditional human faith:

1. Be impeccable with your word.
2. Don't take anything personally.
3. Don't make assumptions.
4. Always do your best.

> API: Assume positive intent—then communicate and act.

We need to do the same in the workplace with millennials: assume the best. Our way at launchbox is to assume positive intent (API).

Let's put your ability to API to the test by considering a few scenarios.

SCENE ONE:
The Millennial and the Meeting
Setting: The office of an industry-leading online bank

Situation: A managers' meeting is about to start. A millennial account executive stops her non-millennial manager as the manager heads to the meeting.

"What's the meeting about?" the account executive asks.

"Nothing you need to worry about," says the manager.

"Can I come?"

"It's just for managers," says the manager, walking toward the conference room, growing annoyed.

"Why? What's it about?" asks the millennial, following the manager to the conference room, growing frustrated.

"Nothing important, just a regular meeting."

"Then, can I come with you?"

"No, it's just for managers."

The manager walks into the meeting annoyed. The millennial stares through the glass walls of the conference room frustrated.

Most people, when considering this scene, relate to either the non-millennial manager or the millennial employee and think the other is absolutely wrong. But they're both wrong, and so are you if you took one side over the other.

Those who side with the managers in this scene instantly see the millennial as entitled and arrogant. This is the foundation for dismissiveness and selfishness. Those glass walls of the conference room underlie a deeper problem that infects too many workplaces today: a false promise of transparency and connection. Walls are walls, even if people can still see each other. Plus, we all know that people in glass houses . . .

Even if this had been a meeting that required some boundaries—employee evaluations, for example—what's the manager's reason for not explaining that to a clearly eager employee? If teaching hospitals let residents into life-or-death situations, what's so important in that meeting that it can't be shared? How would *you* feel looking from the outside in?

Here's what the assumption of entitlement led that manager to dismiss about the millennial.

- She wants to be a part of something.
- She needs to feel appreciated and valued.
- She wants to learn more.
- She believes in transparency.
- She wants to know what her coworkers are doing and how she fits in.

All that from the first short scene? Absolutely.

It is super important that we understand that, because nothing really happens in a vacuum. In fact, what's happening here is even more complicated. I'll let an exceptionally articulate millennial who felt excluded just like the millennial in Scene One explain why.

> Yes, we are all entitled. We see one person do something and we think it's insane that we don't get to also. But I also constantly assume that the reason I don't get to do stuff like that is because I'm not capable. In my head, I come to the obvious conclusions that my bosses don't put the trust in me to do those kinds of things, or it doesn't occur to them to utilize me to do those things because clearly, I can't handle it. That's the exact opposite of entitled. How do we break out of these toxic mindsets?

Who wants employees infected by the toxic doubt that results from ignoring these cravings? I'm not saying the millennial in Scene One did not act entitled or arrogant, or that many millennials don't come across this way. And I am certainly not saying the millennial doesn't need to work on her communication skills. Yeah, there's entitlement there, but who doesn't want to be taught and learn and grow as quickly as possible

Is ambition, even if over the top, *always* a sign of disrespect?

these days? Hasn't the disruptive nature of speed warped the expectations of all of us to get what we want when we want it?

Most millennials don't see it that way, and neither should you. One millennial told me

> Yeah, we want more than we deserve faster than we should. We have gotten things that we want quickly in life. We thrive on instant gratification. We want to be told that we are doing well. That can come off as being pushy or entitled or as poor manners, and it is. But that does not mean I am confident. It is kind of my way of saying I am ready and what I want from a boss: genuine support that will give me confidence to succeed.

Even if the millennial had approached the situation in the best way possible, how many of us would have opened that conference room door, or at least taken the time to explain what was going on? *Try API.* Do we really not want the things these millennials want: inclusion, information, and a chance to learn more?

What is most interesting when we work with millennials at launchbox is that they are more likely than managers to get that they are complicit in the communication gap. They want to listen and grow. Okay, not *all* of them. Focusing only on extremes pushes us back to myths and assumptions. Most millennials accept that they need their managers as much as their managers need them. Millennials know they must learn to have a little more respect and understand there are certain rules of the workspace. (Hey millennials, you work nine-to-five? That means *be there.*) They understand they need to ask for what they want and to make connections. They admit they can't do everything when and how they want to, especially if they need to talk to clients or customers. In fact, most millennials in our launchbox workshops actually *like* being called on the shit they do. It's as if no one ever did that with them before.

Okay, let's try another scene.

SCENE TWO:
The Millennial and the Research Project

Setting: The office of a national engineering and consulting firm

Situation: A non-millennial manager has just given a millennial on his team an assignment to research something of high priority and present what he finds within the hour.

"Sure!" the millennial says as he leaves his manager's office.

The manager watches as the millennial leaves engaged and driven for results and then . . . watches that millennial stop to talk at seemingly every desk and group in the division.

"Holy crap!" the manager thinks. *"Is that guy ever going to get to work and sit down at his computer and do the work to get the assignment done?"*

The manager keeps watching until he can't take it anymore; precious minutes and momentum are being lost. *"I thought he cared,"* the manager thinks anew. He gets up and confronts the millennial.

"What are you doing?"

"What do you mean?"

"What are you doing talking? I *gave* you a priority research assignment. Get back to your desk and do it."

"But . . ."

"No buts," says the manager, who stops the millennial from talking and sends him back to his desk to do the work he was assigned before walking away.

An hour later, the millennial presents the research. Good, but not great, and not what the manager expected of him.

"If only he had focused," thinks the manager.

API is exactly what was missing in this second scene when the manager confronted his millennial on the research project work. When he could not stand what he saw the millennial doing, he made a judgment that assumed negative intent based on the manager's experience: The millennial was not doing the work. So the manager took it personally, stopped the millennial, and made him do the work the way it "should" be done— back to the desk, nose to grindstone. Meanwhile, the millennial wondered, *"Why should I pay your idea of dues when I can deliver better results my way?"*

Is this scenario really evidence that the millennial doesn't deal well with authority? Was he saying "I am not going to do that" or "I am not going to do that *the way you do that*"? The manager points to the subpar work, but the subpar work was actually a self-fulfilling prophecy. What if the manager simply accepted that the millennial just does assignments like these differently? Leaders who realize this may even come to see that the work they get back from millennials is a lot better, *and* produced even faster than they expected, because millennials tap resources, minds, and experience beyond their own.

I'll let a millennial who experienced this exact scene explain it from the millennial side.

The way my manager learns is different from the way I learn. He gives me an assignment and I leave the office and immediately start going and asking questions of people. He looks at me and thinks, "What the heck is wrong with that kid? He's wasting his time talking to everybody while I've given him an assignment! Why is he not building a spreadsheet or researching?" I see it as how I learn, how I was taught to gather information: Ask the people who have knowledge about this what they think the best way to handle it is before I do the research so I do not waste time. He is making a judgment that I am a dumbass and not following his directions, and most importantly, that I'm not going to get done what he needs me to get done. Yet I am actually getting exactly what he needs done, just my way.

Here's what this manager's assumptions led him to dismiss about his millennial in Scene Two.

- He has been exposed to different thinking and approaches than the manager.
- He desires teamwork.
- He seeks out collaboration.
- He sees value in other people who may have done something similar and asks them questions about it.

Yes, with one small but important action, this manager stood in the way of all that, all because he equated his expectations of how the work should be done with his expectations for the work itself. *"This is the way I did it when I started and how it has always been done. The culture is what it is,"* he thinks, which sounds to me like: *"When I was your age, we never collaborated. We sat alone in an office with no heat and a single bulb, stayed late, and never complained. We had no food and water and needed to walk home . . ."*

Millennials are into self-discovery, and one of the things they discover working with us is how to make their managers manage them well to make them perform well. They also get that they have to break through their own myths and assumptions about the previous generations— that they are arrogant know-it-alls; they don't care about their teams/people/clients; they don't care about recognition; they're only in it for the money; they fear nontraditional approaches; they are inflexible and stuck in their ways; and they don't like change. Well, that last one is true about most of us.

In this case, however, I have the benefit of being a perennial millennial. I have an unwavering focus on youth and the benefit and perspective that young people have brought and continue to bring to the world, which emanates from my lifelong journey and passion to help people be their best. While most non-millennial leaders see millennials as scattered, I see them as collaborative. They see them as needy; I see them as craving feedback. Sure, some of what millennials expect and feel entitled to is unrealistic, like wanting to go from the mailroom to the boardroom in a day. But is that *only* entitlement, or are they opportunistic, ambitious, and giving us a sign that business is changing as well?

Yes, I think millennials have as much to learn as non-millennials and are complicit in many of the problems they face, but I prefer to API. I really like what young people are about: hope, promise, innovation, future, learning, wanting to grow, and all those crazy messages in their heads. They are only trying to make sense of all this craziness as four seemingly very different generations bump into each other in the workplace. Millennials are the largest of these generations, and they are the ones pushing the proverbial envelope *and* non-millennials' proverbial buttons. So most of us push back (yes, I am guilty of this, too), refusing to acknowledge that the world is different today and clinging to "the way things have always been." But we can show them we are trying by busting those myths.

Okay, it's your turn to get a new view. Let's test what you learned by challenging your assumptions and your ability to API about one of the most commented on aspects about millennials.

SCENE THREE:
The Millennial and the Headphones
Setting: The office of a major public relations and marketing business

Situation: The non-millennial boss walks in and through the office, shouting hellos as she goes. She gets a bunch of hellos back, and strikes up a few conversations along the way. But she can't help but notice that half her team have their headphones on already and a few don't even hear her greeting.

"What is it about those $#!& headphones. They are always on, right?" she says to no one but herself as she makes her way to the office.

Sitting at her desk, she can't let it go. *"They are on when they arrive in the morning. They are on in the office all day,"* she steams. *"I feel they are so disconnected from the office. They are tuning me out. They don't answer emails, won't answer voice mails, and only text and tweet; they couldn't have a conversation if I paid them to, and I am paying them. But those damned headphones . . ."*

Eventually, she lets it go until she heads to the gym before lunch and spots one of her millennials working out . . . with her headphones on. She doesn't even bother to wave and takes out her anger on the exercise bike.

"I go to the gym to make connections and be social while I work out; they're tuning out this opportunity," she yells to herself. *"This is proof they are in their own world and expect me to ignore it and deal with it. They have headphones on when they leave for the day and probably on when they go to bed."*

She decides to ban headphones in the office for all but phone calls and listening to work-related material.

What do you think of what this boss was saying and feeling, and her solution to the problem? Before you react, think back to the previous scenarios: What are some of her assumptions about this employee? Take a moment and think, *"What's the other side of the story?"* Ask yourself

- What are the boss's assumptions?
- What is the millennial perspective?
- What if the manager had assumed positive intent?
- How would you handle this situation?

To be honest, no one would have any difficulty understanding how someone would say things like these, let alone me. I may be Mr. Millennial, but the gym is a place where I make a considerable number of personal and client connections. Ninety percent of my initial business at launchbox came from the gym where I work out, and half the people at my wedding worked out with my wife and me. I have trouble understanding why anyone would wear headphones there.

So what if you went to the gym and you saw one of your millennial employees working out with his headphones on, oblivious to you and anyone else who might be a potential connection? How can you expect that millennial to make a connection with others and make relationships when they can't even be social at the gym? You can't really blame the boss for being upset, right?

Well, this one is more complicated than it seems, because millennials put on headphones both to stay connected *and* to set boundaries. Headphones in the office are part of that connection, but headphones elsewhere can mean something else. Consider what this millennial says about his boss being upset with him because he wears those headphones all the time, especially at the gym.

> I work out at the gym with my headphones on because the gym is where I tune out with music and recharge. My managers see it as selfish, but I will answer a text at 3:00 a.m. if I have to. I am almost always connected. I just don't *want* to be connected at the gym. I'm wearing headphones in the office *because I always need to be connected there and everywhere else.* In the gym, I just want twenty minutes of release to reset and tune out, resolve issues, think, and plan. I get that's where the previous generations make [personal] connections, and I want connection, too. But if you want to connect and build a relationship with me, ask me to lunch. I would love to talk to you. If you must, you can ask me to work out with you, too, but don't expect me to do it as a rule.

How'd you do? Did you anticipate the complication and some of what this millennial said before he said it? Considered from both sides, who seems the more disconnected here? The facts are on the side of the millennial in terms of what he said (at least I haven't seen a survey that contradicts it yet). According to the U.S. Chamber of Commerce Foundation's *Millennial Generation Research Review*: "Millennials are never far away from their next text, with 80 percent sleeping with their cell phone next to the bed."

In the end, what would happen if you changed some of your assumptions about the headphones being a source of *disconnect* before you next see them on your millennials?

After considering these scenes and everything else in this chapter, I hope you have at least contemplated that millennials—and indeed others in general—might not always be what you assume them to be. It's all about busting myths by shifting to a mindset that puts positive intent into action intent. That's how you get out of your own way and knock down walls of preconceived notions and judgments that prevent us from seeing beyond what we *think* we know.

> Communication is the challenge and the solution.

Millennials just want a fair workplace that values what they offer and plots a path for their success. When they get it, they tend to stick around. Problem is, most companies have no idea what millennials care about. Don't wear your millennial myth lens and cling to the dark side of negativity: focus on and ASSUME POSITIVE INTENT. Replace "but" with "and"—collaborate to create solutions. Who cares if it is not the way you did it or it has always been done? Give it up. It's not relevant.

MAKE IT HAPPEN:
I Understand Disconnects and Bust Myths

I have spent a lifetime working tirelessly to break through my tendency to live in judgment, create quick opinions, and be overly critical. Seeing others first with understanding and meaning has been step one in creating a great marriage, advisory board, friend network, business, and team that works much more seamlessly. It makes all those things easier and way more fun.

What can you do tomorrow to "breakthrough" and break through myths and start assuming positive intent? Remember: One size does not fit all.

1. **Breakthrough generational stereotypes.** Don't make assumptions when dealing with other generations—we are more the same than different.

2. **Make an effort to understand and value different work needs, values, and styles.** Take an interest in others and they will take an interest in you. Remember to ask: Is it more important how they do something or the results they get doing it?.

3. **Focus on and assume positive intent.** Practice the act of understanding through communication. When confronted with something you don't understand, ask "What is their motivation? What do I think they want to achieve? What is their intent? Is this my issue or theirs? What do I want to achieve?" Communication is the challenge *and* the solution.

R: Real Deal

Create real-deal, authentic, caring relationships with your team.

#authenticity

I first notice it as we leave the parking garage. We have just arrived at my wife's company's holiday party at a nearby hotel and casino, and as we head inside from the garage, the first employee who sees us lifts his head and gives us a huge smile. Then we pass a gentleman sweeping the floor, and he does the same thing.

Now I know something is going on, so I say to Danielle, "Watch this. Watch what happens." We walk past the front desk of the hotel where about a dozen people are working, and as soon as I catch their eyes, one by one they all look up and give us huge smiles. I mean warm and genuine feel-good smiles. It's like a wave of smiles as we pass.

Of course, I am thinking about this throughout the party, and when it ends, I tell Danielle I have to play some more. And so we leave in the opposite direction we came in from and sure enough, the same thing happens. I head back to the front desk and find the manager and ask her, "What is going on with this place? How do you train your people? This is unreal. Amazing. I train people for a living and I want to know what you do. All my clients need to know this."

"We take this very seriously," she says. "It's called 'Everyone Greets Everyone.'"

It totally worked to communicate the message the hotel wants, which is quite impressive, because according to results from an Interact/Harris Poll, 91 percent of employees say communication issues prevent effective leadership. In the survey, reported in *Harvard Business Review* (*http://bit .ly/1TNdSJM*), employees called out communication issues that point to a striking lack of emotional intelligence and the wrong mindset among business leaders. These issues include micromanaging, bullying, narcissism, indecisiveness, and more—all of which prevent leaders from being effective.

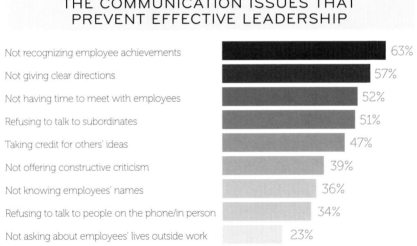

THE COMMUNICATION ISSUES THAT PREVENT EFFECTIVE LEADERSHIP

Not recognizing employee achievements	63%
Not giving clear directions	57%
Not having time to meet with employees	52%
Refusing to talk to subordinates	51%
Taking credit for others' ideas	47%
Not offering constructive criticism	39%
Not knowing employees' names	36%
Refusing to talk to people on the phone/in person	34%
Not asking about employees' lives outside work	23%

Problem is, what we perceive as good communication is anything but good, largely because for most of us, communication is a one-way street: We talk at each other, not to each other. This may work to short-term effect (especially in arguments and politics), but good relationships—

the most important life/work skill—and the success we gain from them personally and professionally depend upon us making good communication a reality. Not so easy when you can get any information, product, or service you want right now through that smartphone sitting beside you, never interacting or connecting with another human being. Which is why, from the rest of us, communication and a caring personality is what millennials need. Millennials and indeed all people *expect* that from their leaders and the brands/companies they support. They want to be cared about and we need to communicate that beyond a drive-by comment of "I care." They want and need us to share our strengths, stories, and experiences and then allow them to do the same with us, which is why we need to be thoughtful and present every day and in every conversation in the most genuine way possible. And the only way to do that is to be strong enough and comfortable enough in our own skins to give up making it about *us*.

Do you have this kind of real, caring, authentic relationships with your team, customers, and clients? I had someone in a workshop come up to me and say, "I am a great actor." What he meant is he acts like he cares. How well do you think that works in this world, today? Even if you are the best actor, it does not work that well. That is playing, people. You care for people by being genuinely interested in them and their well-being. So how can you care inauthentically? *Inauthentic caring is an oxymoron.*

> Do you seek to understand? Get interested now!

Simply put, you *can* communicate with and lead people who have different approaches to work if you value difference—if you share but listen, have a clear vision but ask lots of questions, and be a leader who is also a servant to your people. You *can't* communicate and lead in business or culture by being self-absorbed and by stifling individuality. That's the way to inauthenticity and irrelevance.

Instead, master the following real-deal steps for opening yourself up to others to form the relationships you need.

✓ **Connect authentically.** Create real emotional connections by showing genuine interest and care for your team's personal well-being.

✓ **Share yourself.** Let others see and know the real you.

✓ **Know the power of the question.** Understand needs, motivators, and challenges, and then be willing to have tough conversations around that understanding.

✓ **Show gratitude.** Be thankful for what you've got. And never forget to say "Thanks!"

Be warned: If you freaked out about doing the "soft stuff" in the first part of this book, hold onto your hat, because you're going to take that soft stuff to a new level here and use it to connect with your people beyond the work at hand.

Connect

I am not a perfect leader—or person—by any stretch of the imagination. My company, like every company I have worked for and all companies out there, has problems and issues. I will screw up, as will my people. But if I create a culture that encourages authentic leadership and wants everyone to be and share who they are? I will still have a great reputation, high morale, strong productivity, and continued loyalty from my people and my customers—even when there's nothing but bad news on the books.

How far are you willing to go to achieve this?

I have a friend who worked at the Sony headquarters in San Diego who told me that in 2010, the new head of the electronics business stopped by her desk to say hello. Now, my friend wasn't a high-ranking officer, nor was the president treating her as special; he stopped by *every* desk on her floor and the entire ten-story tower.

"Crazy," she thought. So she asked why. He told her he wanted to share a little about who he was to show them he cared about and valued

them they way he cared about and valued his family, which he explained was the single most important thing in his life. It didn't take but a few minutes for that president at Sony to get his ball of authenticity rolling through the company, though I hear it took him days to complete his meetings from bottom floor to top. *Days*. That's awesome commitment to authentic connection. This guy did not *act* interested—he *was* interested. He asked questions, because he

> It's not just about what you *do*. It's about showing who you *are*.

wanted to know the answers. As a result, everyone bottom to top knew who he was on some level and genuinely felt they had a relationship. He kept meeting with them, too, in town hall–style meetings. And when Sony went through some difficult layoffs in the next years, my friend's team's morale stayed surprisingly high.

To wade into the waters of authenticity on this level, first you need to answer this question honestly: *Are you a different person personally and professionally?* If so, stop that right now. To be the real deal, the line between the personal and professional must be erased.

Everything you do can be looked on suspiciously if it is not done genuinely and authentically as one "you." Why do you even need to be a different person? What is the point? Millennials see right through poseurs who pretend to care because they think they *should* be caring. And while the line between business and personal has perhaps forever been blurred by millennials, managers should be adept at calling out those millennials who refuse to open up genuinely as well.

I'm not saying you can't be a *private* person—privacy is okay; I'm not into oversharing. There are lines, though those lines tend to move from company to company. I'm talking about being the same authentic person in public and in private. Authenticity has *power*. I'm not sure if it is because of fear that we don't show who we really are and deliver our stories. Maybe we have lost the tools and we need consultants like me to find them. Maybe we are still in denial that authenticity has power, because decades of leadership training taught the previous generations that you couldn't communicate and show who you truly are *and* be successful.

And I am probably the umpteen-thousandth person to say this to you. Like sunscreen, we seem to know we should wear authenticity every day, but we seem to forget its importance. And then we get burned. Sometimes really badly. Getting burned too badly leads to "cancer" in a business. I've *had* cancer. It sucks.

Remember: The inverse of authenticity is dishonesty. The inverse of trust is lying. See the connection? Don't say what you think you should be, say, or do. Say what you actually believe, even if it is unpopular or tough or feels uncomfortable. Treating this all as a bunch of new tricks and techniques to add to a self-centered foundation will result in failure.

This is where you must remember your story and your personal brand words. They are as real as you get. Own them in an open and honest way and you will be perceived as real and genuine and take a huge step toward permanently establishing communication and trust.

Share Yourself

As I was writing this book, Stacey, one of my right hands at launchbox, told me I should share the story about a nosebleed I had while skiing in Deer Valley. She said, "When you share personal info like that, it makes other people feel more comfortable sharing with you, which was true for me and I'm sure others you told."

Funny thing is, I couldn't remember the story. Not because I was making it up or anything to do with who Stacey is, but because I share stories like this every day to help people know me, make people comfortable (or uncomfortable, if that is my goal), and encourage them to share back, because sharing equals connecting. *Sharing must be the rule, not the exception.* It shows vulnerability—which always come from strength despite being painted as a weakness.

We cannot be afraid to do this! We cannot close ourselves off. No more getting in elevators and not saying a word or acknowledging anyone is there. The days of mixing and mingling only at company outings and holiday parties are so twentieth-century.

Vulnerability is essential to allow our stories and experiences to shine as we share.

People who work for me know my whole story (which I told in Part One), and I compel them to write and share theirs. That fires us up, building a passion for working together to achieve our goals and get our business where it needs to go. That's real connection, which leads to contribution.

There's an old adage that people quit their bosses, not their jobs. That may or may not be true. Prospects for advancement, compensation, lack of trust and respect, and poor work/life balance also place at or near the top of many surveys on why people leave. What is indisputable is that the number one reason people *stay* in their jobs is because of their bosses: *You* are the most important person in determining turnover, because you have the ability to build the relationships that connect with your people, empower them, and create a culture of success and results. And nothing builds momentum for change within companies more than results.

- **STOP** making excuses for not spending enough time thinking about and connecting to your people.

- **START** being genuinely interested in and showing respect for your team members as people; understanding what motivates them; creating and supporting career advancement paths and opportunities; and acting on their issues and concerns.

What are some things we can do as managers to get real and show we care to form relationships?

First Step: Learn

Build on the work from the inside out and put your finger on the pulse of your people by proactively learning things about them and what matters to them. Enabling millennials (and indeed anyone) to answer questions about themselves, what they think, what they know, and how they perceive the world in front of them opens them up and makes them receptive to what you have to say.

- **Ask who they are.** Where are you from? What do you do for fun? What makes you get out of bed in the morning? What was the best thing that happened to you last year?
- **Ask what they do and how they are feeling.** Do you drink coffee to stay awake? Did you go to the gym? Did you have a good day? How was your weekend?
- **Ask how they use their strengths.** What are you good at? What do your friends and family say you are good at? What do others at the company rely on you for?

EXERCISE:

"If You Really Knew Me, You Would Know . . ."

For the inexperienced, uninitiated, or those looking for new ways to start sharing with one another, try this with your team.

1. Everyone forms one big circle.
2. Pick one person. That person and then every second person takes a step forward, creating an inner circle.
3. The inner circle faces the outer circle.
4. Each person greets the person in front of him or her and both take turns finishing the statement, "If you really knew me, you would know . . ."

5. When both turns are done, the inner circle moves clockwise by one, while the outer circle stands still.

6. Repeat from step four until everyone on the inner circle has shared with everyone on the outside. The *only* rule about what you share is you have to use a new piece of information each time you move to a new person until you have spoken to at least five people.

Granted, these things are easier to do when you have a smaller company and can control the sharing yourself. In larger and rapidly growing companies, the people responsible for individual teams must do this with their teams, and there must be clearly defined processes and procedures that value caring and require making the time for sharing a condition of employment. That's how you establish a culture of connection and engagement across a company. You can then use that connection to make sure your people know you and understand your expectations of them.

Second Step: Give It Time

What always costs leaders in sharing and exercises like this is a lack of ability to prioritize making connections with their employees. To connect with people requires time. In a 140-character world, this may be the most contrarian thing you can do—and thus the most real: *Give your people your time*. That's why managers don't like to do it. We just want to tell people what to do, not learn more about them. We must learn to make time for sharing with others and caring enough to learn more about them.

Third Step: Actually *Listen* to the Answers

Active listening is an often-overlooked skill in exhibiting business acumen. There is nothing worse than feeling like you are being asked a question by a person who doesn't seem to care about the answer.

You must

- be present
- be genuinely curious
- be caring and concerned
- show respect and keep quiet
- strive to help the question asker

ACTIVE LISTENING BEHAVIORS

DOS	DON'TS
Keep quiet	Give advice
Lean in—ears, eyes, heart	Assume or judge
Pay attention to body language and emotions	React emotionally
	Be planning your response
Seek to understand, paraphrase back	Ask leading questions
Ask open-ended questions to learn more	

Active listening shows respect, not just when it comes to questions but in any conversation. The dos and don'ts are pretty straightforward.

Active listening is *not* about being silent. It is about refraining from judgment and thinking about your own response while the other person is speaking, and then more using questions to clarify and expand understanding for both sharer and listener. That's the power the best questions have.

Know the Power of the Question

When we were on a family vacation in Alaska, my daughter, Allie, asked the experts at Seavey's Dog Sledding if the same dogs always lead and the others go in the same position each time. The answer from Seth the Master Musher was masterful: Every race thousands of inputs and factors can determine why the dogs go where and when. The situation determines the leaders, which requires the person running the whole thing to have both awareness of the situation *and* awareness of the team. "Leaders must have deep connections to the dogs to succeed and make sure the dogs are connected to each other," he said.

Not very different when it comes to leading people.

I learned how much we have lost the art of asking questions after my son Zach graduated from college. As we prepared him and a friend who had also just graduated for their interviews, I started rattling off the things they needed to do, from the handshake to the written thank-you. When I started in on how to make it about others, and the best questions to ask, such as: What would success look like in this job? What would indicate that I am doing a really good job? What . . . Zach and his friend cut me off. "Slow down; they don't teach us any of this in school!"

None of it—and he was in a *business* school.

As I wrote in the introduction, I was already well aware that my son (a millennial graduate of a *Wall Street Journal* national Top 25 prep school and a top business school) and his friend (a graduate of a top liberal arts college)—along with nearly 100 percent of their peers—had never been taught the value of understanding what their strengths are; articulating their skills, passions, and values, and what they want their brands to be in the world; and developing and delivering their stories. But if no one is teaching them the power of questions, *no one is teaching them the essential tool for building relationships and connecting with human beings.*

It is up to us, the non-millennials, to relearn this forgotten art and then coach the millennials on retaining, practicing, and exercising it. We should be trained like lawyers questioning witnesses, to draw them out and share. Strive to make every question you ask one that cannot be answered with a yes or no. (Don't ask

> Question asking takes us off our mark, down from our soapbox, away from our self-centered ways.

"Did you read the materials the client gave us?" but "What did you think of our clients' materials?") You should want your millennials to do the same—to ask and answer good questions constantly to create understanding: What could I be doing more and better? How does what I am doing fit in? That's how you balance millennials' need for individuality and value the individual, while still respecting the overall mission and work of the company.

Here's the easiest way to learn or relearn how to do this and shift from self- to other-centered: *In every encounter with someone you want to influence, challenge yourself to ask him or her five to ten questions before opening your mouth to say something about you.*

How amazing would it be if one of the rules of your company was "Ask five provocative questions of your people before you tell them what to do"? I practice this as a rule. In fact, I strive to ask people *twenty* questions about themselves, because people like talking about themselves. If I am entering a new potential relationship, I research every part of the person and company that I can. If I don't have the time, I look for visual clues to find the questions to ask to find commonality or make a connection—what's in the room or office when I enter it? What do I see? Are there pictures? Anything interesting? Something I haven't seen before? Something I covet?

With companies growing in size and complexity, it is essential that leaders do this. We can do this by reminding millennials of their importance and relation to the organization as a whole by frequently asking questions like "How does this relate to our broader vision and mission?" This is why companies like Zappos, Southwest, and Red Robin broadcast their operating values so publicly and

> Great questions are open-ended, nonjudgmental, and supportive.

compel their leaders to ask "How is what we are doing aligning with our core operating values?" There is no confusion as to what those values are. It not only makes decision making easier and less contentious, but also establishes a deeper alignment and connection between manager and millennials and binds them to the organization's mission.

Asking questions makes us smarter, more interested and interesting, and present—it gives us the ability to influence. In business, questions are how we reach inside others and ourselves to learn and

- **draw others into the conversation:** What do you think about that? Does this tap into your experience? Have you seen something like this before? What can we learn here? What are the goals and objectives?
- **understand needs, motivators, and challenges:** How can I make it easier for you? How can I help you do that? What do you need from me to be successful? What unexpected obstacles might we anticipate?
- **tune into nonverbals in order to formulate more supportive questions:** Do you sense hesitation or dread in your employee's voice? Ask them what they are going through, sensing, dreading . . .
- **encourage more questions to push your people to solve problems, innovate, and take risks—and be willing to accept the resulting tension:** Be a constructive provocateur. Here's what that sounds like: "Why? . . . Love that question, great question! That was provocative! Go with that! . . . What else do you think? . . . Interesting! Help me understand that point of view more . . . What will happen if this doesn't work? What could/ should we do if that happens?"

That last point is essential because it helps us have the tough conversations we would prefer to avoid. And by avoiding direct real-deal conversations, we give away so much power—power we could use to help ourselves connect and help teams band together to make a difference. Being unable or even unwilling to communicate in that way quashes impact and influence. It equals succumbing to what is hard, and not pushing yourself and those around you to confront problems and test limits to come up with bold, powerful solutions together.

Take this story as an example of the many tough conversations that happen daily. I was talking to a woman whose adult daughter was moving home after failing out of rehab—again—and she was concerned that moving home would just enable her daughter's habit. I asked her if she had a contract with her daughter about the rules of the house, work she needs to do, whether she needs to pay rent . . . The woman shrugged me off. "Just give me the name of a coach for her and a therapist." She said she was not worried about the contract. Why? "Because that's easy to do."

I called BS on that; if it were easy, she'd have that contract. She was doing anything to avoid or delay the tough conversation, including hiring someone else to have it for her. So would many of us. And it is no different at the office. Not that many of us are good at the hard conversations anywhere in life, but there are basic rules for having tough and direct conversations from the very beginning that draw on your new real-deal skills.

RULES FOR TOUGH CONVERSATIONS

1. Identify the problem.
2. Attack the problem, not each other.
3. Listen to others' points of view, and acknowledge them.
4. Focus on organizational goals and objectives.
5. Listen as an ally to strategize for success.

Again: simple, but not easy to do. If it were, I wouldn't have watched an entire team I was brought in to coach at a billion-dollar company nearly fall apart because there was no place for sharing and questioning and thus having direct and tough conversations about the good and the bad—not from the manager to his millennials nor the millennials to their leader.

This leader was a hard and autocratic woman who had come up through the ranks as a woman in a man's world. She had been brought in with a single mandate: refocus the business and grow the team substantially. Her goal was to get her team to work together and function in pursuit of this growth mission, and we soon had the team winning more contracts just based on our inside-out work. But they were still not performing at the capacity I knew they could, and I was pretty sure why: the leader.

When I tried to have a conversation about how the team felt about the leader and what she was telling them to do, all of them went silent. These people had no idea how to talk to one another about anything but the baseline terms laid out by the leader. They were scared to say any more. They just could not find a way to share what they wanted to say to her: "We love you and you are a really good person, but we are kind of scared of you."

How can you ask for what you need when you are too scared or don't feel empowered to ask—and no one is modeling that behavior?

We all know what happens when people become this unhappy: They leave. We like to think it is some movie where everyone hugs it out to an uplifting pop soundtrack. This ain't the movies. And there is a *bigger* problem that happens before they leave: People become disengaged, care less, and become less productive. And as we learned, disengagement is a major problem for businesses in general and explains why the team was not performing at capacity. They didn't like what was going on, but what could they do? They had gotten comfortable not saying anything and were too frightened of the tough conversation to say what they felt.

I tried to force this conversation in our next meeting with the team and the leader. She was making a presentation and ended with a bold, proud assessment directed at them: how great it had been since she had been here; how they were moving in the right direction; and how she was pleased they all felt comfortable talking with her. They were all silent. So I opened my mouth because they couldn't, and asked a question of the team: Do they really think things are great? How do you feel? How do you feel about what she just said?

And much to my shock and delight, they actually told her.

"I don't really feel comfortable talking to you."

"I don't really know where you are coming from."

"Your plan isn't really helping me see the light and I can't find the space to ask any questions."

"I don't think I can talk to you about anything except on your autocratic terms, because the culture of this team doesn't allow me to."

You get the picture.

Holy hell.

By failing to have the tough conversations, this leader got blindsided by these responses and disconnects and the drama she didn't expect or need. To say that fireworks went off after these revelations would be an understatement.

First, the leader went nuts that her team didn't trust her. She was disappointed. She was pissed—at the team *and* me. "What's wrong with you guys?" she screamed. That's what she heard: *They* were the problem. You are with me or against me—on my team or not on my team—and "with me" equals trust.

To be sure, not a single person in that room was acting authentically, genuinely, or honestly. I wanted to yell at them, "Man and woman up! Be the real deal and own what is happening." But what if I had? It is not like the leader was listening or curious about what they were saying. She was complicit in their pent-up frustration: She didn't want to see anything that she didn't want to, or know anything but results.

> Have an insatiable curiosity.

It was a big mess. All because this leader did not care, share, ask questions, or follow the rules for having direct and tough conversations. The point isn't that this leader's style was "tough as nails" and "hard ass." You can be an authentic hard ass, showing how tough you are. The point is she gave them no space and showed no interest in her team saying anything but what she wanted to hear. She had not created an environment where sharing and openness were permitted and valued. While they trusted her, she wasn't earning their trust and making it about them. As a result, the truth never got out there, trust got undermined, and authentic connections were devalued.

There is more to learn to create a sustainable culture that supports having direct and tough conversations. For now, you only need to listen to me and hear that nothing in business is just about you anymore. It's not about "them" either. Millennials want what we all should want: sheer honesty and realism.

In the end, this leader accepted what the team and I said, even though she found it hard to change. I appreciated that she came to trust me and respected that I cared enough to tell her the truth and get the truth out there, and that I was in her face, real, and authentic. But I knew she was struggling to understand that this was exactly what she did not allow her team to be. If this leader had just valued communication by knowing and deploying the influence of sharing and listening, and the power of questions, she could have enabled her team to do the same and avoided having her problems grow like snowballs into avalanches of nonsense.

As I stated before, this leader's difficulty with tough conversations and questions—not caring enough to ask them herself or encouraging her millennials to ask them of her—is not unique. Many leaders assume that they are giving all their power away by engaging their people to be curious and by rewarding those who ask questions, act provocatively, and take risks. It appears weak, like they are not in control. But it is actually the opposite. This leader would have so much more power and influence if she had engaged her people, asked questions, and listened to *their* questions to understand what they wanted and needed. And if she had then taken all the amazing energy that resulted to enlist them in creating solutions and a deep sense of shared commitment and trust. Caring enough to communicate that way shows confidence—it gives you power by valuing others. Not doing that gives power away and devalues your team.

That's what great communication does. It makes people feel valued. Here's another way: Just care enough to demonstrate gratitude and say, "Thank you," in each and every way possible all the time.

Show Gratitude

Remember that myth from the last chapter about millennials being high maintenance and requiring feedback all the time? ("Please tell me how great I am. Every day. Twice.") Not a myth. The myth is that they want us to tell them this because they think they are special or entitled. Honestly, we should understand this need for positive feedback.

First of all, we all occasionally indulge in a little of what the Urban Dictionary calls "humblebragging": subtly letting others know about how fantastic your life is while undercutting it with a bit of self-effacing humor or woe-is-me gloss. ("Ugh, I just ate about fifteen pieces of chocolate and warm cookies in first class. I gotta learn to control myself or next time I'll puke all over that supermodel #humblebrag.")

Second of all, we are all guilty of doing a little bit of actual bragging now and then. As a matter of fact, sharing how great our lives are can be part of real-deal connecting—or an entry to it. Was it hard to listen to the guys on the chairlift talking about how NetJets is expensive and private jets are great if you know how to do it, as we made our way up the slopes? Absolutely. But after the next run they actually told me about how grateful they were at being able to help their employees grow and shape their careers, and then asked me how they could help others. They went from #humblebrag to brag to demonstrating gratitude and humility—all in two chairlift rides.

We *all* have the expectation of being able to connect with people— and sometimes we even feel entitled to do so with all our good things and accomplishments. So tell me why are we so leery about doing it? Do we think it makes us narcissists? No, narcissists share the good, but it is all about them—they almost always forget to be humble and thus equally if not more grateful to others as well.

It is imperative that you learn how to share stories about yourself, even the good stuff, and communicate them authentically, honestly, productively, and constructively—but then show humility and use them to show gratitude.

To do this well requires understanding the actual definition of gratitude: the quality of being thankful; readiness to show appreciation for and to return kindness. To honor this definition on an authentic level requires first and foremost the humility of understanding. That understanding comes through day-to-day connection, sharing, and the question asking we just covered. It then requires you to be humble enough to actually be thankful. What is more beautiful than a child who is loving and grateful to his or her parents, or a husband who adores and thanks his wife? Nothing. We love it. We want to attract people and situations like this personally. Shouldn't we want this in ourselves professionally? Isn't that how we will eventually get it in return?

We have a duty to model to the people on our team how we expect them to manage and work with other employees, coworkers, their peers, and us. Only then can we bring in real, authentic storytelling as part of a system for delivering value and empowering success. People who tell stories with gratitude attract you and let you know how special they are without any bragging (humble or otherwise). They make you *feel* like you should connect with them. They embody all the attributes that millennials (and most people) want in relationships and are most attracted to. So show some gratitude—being careful to make it authentic—and make others around you feel it.

> What are the two most powerful words in the workplace? Not "Yes, sir" or "Yes, ma'am," but "Thank you."

How do we carefully show that gratitude? To get started, ask yourself: *Do I really know how to show gratitude and say "thank you?"* (Not just "thank you" to the person who holds the door open or who brings your food.) The answer is probably "No, not enough."

A great thank-you is the easiest, most powerful way to build relation-ships with your employees, customers, and prospects. In fact, most mil-lennials are more motivated by a genuine thank-you note than a reward for good work. How's that for increasing results and profits? That's a *power thank-you.*

A POWER THANK-YOU IS

1. **TIMELY.** Do it *now*; give recognition freely and in the moment.

2. **ABOUT THEM,** not you.

3. **SPECIFIC.** "Good job" isn't enough—tell them what they did and why it was important.

4. **PERSONAL, REAL,** and **CONNECTIVE.**

It should also be habitual. Too many leaders have this prevailing sense that feedback has to be negative. No! To bridge the gap in a real and authentic way we only need to *make feedback more balanced to the caring side.*

We can't just go do the work and be critical about the process and results. I love it and thank people when they give me their mindshare—what could be more important? We can't be so driven and take ourselves so seriously that we cannot celebrate where and who we are and what we've done well. Have we forgotten what Ken Blanchard told us in his classic *The One Minute Manager*? "Catch them doing something right." That only takes a minute! Do we need to be reminded what Tom Rath said in his best-selling book *How Full Is Your Bucket?*: that your smallest interactions deeply affect others, and the frequency of them is essential to productivity and morale (Rath's "magic ratio" is five positive interac-tions for every negative interaction). What's your excuse?

You can't overpraise—millennials have a solid BS meter—so the key is balance. Remember: The goal of feedback should be constructive improvement. Show that you care and believe in them and their capabilities for change and growth. Learn to check in with employees to demonstrate care about them and what they are doing. Millennials expect positive *and* productive feedback. They want to know how they are doing, especially when they are doing well.

So coach them and tell them what they need to improve, but also share what you love.

Take the thank-you challenge all day, every day.

- Identify who you need to thank.
- Express real, personal, meaningful gratitude for each person's unique contributions in your business and your personal life.
- Thank them with specifically crafted bullets that let them know you appreciate them and the mindshare they gave you.
- Do it *now*, not when things are "less crazy"; they never are.
- Swing for the fences for a response that says "that was the best thank-you I have ever received."

My story from the first part of this book is not only about recognizing the community that I want to help, but also about how they have helped me. Go back and look at your story and look around your office and ask yourself, *"When was the last time I said thank you without needing something? When was the last time I had no ulterior motive for some public display of thoughtfulness?"* Too long? Trust me, people notice. Maybe pick up the phone and reconnect. Tell them. Be known for giving great thank-yous.

> Say thank you and give praise for all of the good things your people do, every day.

Send a note. Stop by their offices. Send a book. Have lunch together. Do more than Snapchat, Instagram, or text. Even if it is a millennial.

MAKE IT HAPPEN:
I Commit to Real-Deal Connecting and Caring

What can you do tomorrow to create authentic, caring relationships? What are you doing to be relevant and be the real deal? Great managers bridge the gap by being thoughtful and present—that is how they manifest personal relevance and remain relevant to their stakeholders. They really connect and care authentically by showing gratitude and expressing your value. To become great, we must make our people, not us, the heroes of our business stories. Remember: Relationships are the most important life/work skill, and you must be the real deal to build authentic, caring relationships. So what can you do tomorrow to create authentic, caring relationships? Become other-directed or other-centric.

1. **Connect authentically** and **care more** and enough to get interested. Show respect for your team members as people. You can't fake it; they see through it.
2. **Share yourself.** Create emotional connections through sharing your story and experiences, showing your personality and strengths; let others see and know the real you.
3. **Know the power of the question.** Ask how you can help and *mean it.* Ask at least ten tough and provocative open-ended questions each day before you do anything else.
4. **Show gratitude and express it** in every interaction. Really share—even the good stuff—but don't forget: humility rules.

The benefits of investing time to create real, authentic caring relationships will be well worth it in engagement, loyalty, and results. Make your people feel good by understanding what motivates them; creating and supporting career advancement paths and opportunities; and acting on issues and concerns.

I: I Own It

Own personal responsibility and accountability to drive results.

#controlyourself

After being with the same woman for thirty-two years, I would be lying if I told you we haven't been to a therapist. And I am grateful we did, if only because our therapist, Lorie, gave me the best line that I have ever heard about accountability—a line I use all the time with everyone I coach: *If you want change and want to change, clean your side of the street first.*

Cleaning your side of the street is about owning your own shit before asking someone to own theirs. Which means, perhaps ironically, that making it about you is one of the most other-directed things you can do. Your street-sweeping ownership builds on the solid foundation of the inside-out work you did in Part One, especially

> What do you own? Clean your side of the street first.

your strengths and story, and being your best self first. Let me tell you, it really changes your perspective by forcing you to become humble and self-aware enough to own what you are doing first, to make things better. By asking *"What am I going to do to change and address this problem or situation?"* If you do that, you both win. And we have.

Cleaning your side of the street means the same thing in professional life as it does in personal life: *Turn the spotlight on yourself first when problems arise.*

- *Don't ask:* What did that person do? What bothers me about another person—millennial or otherwise—at work, at home, or anywhere in between? What are they going to do to change and own that problem?
- *Do ask:* What did I do to cause this mess? What can I do to own responsibility and come to the table with a solution? What I can do to help, make it better, and get results?

The goal in cleaning your side of the street is for each side to become "clean"—both aware of their responsibilities, seeing themselves as complicit in the divide, and working to create the workplaces they want and need. None of that happens if everyone refuses to act and lets the "dirt" just keep piling up.

Take this story of a young millennial working at a growing fifty-person technology firm where I had the privilege to serve at the C-level as a senior leader. The millennial, who was at the company before I started, worked hard. She pushed her way through each and every opportunity. She was a star with a can-do attitude who gave it her all and really showed up every day. But the company was a totally challenging environment that eventually eroded her eagerness. The rest of the C-suite was tough—and I mean *really* tough—but even more disgusting, they just egged this poor millennial on, dangling carrot after proverbial carrot with success always just out of reach.

Soon the millennial got tired of broken promises, shattered dreams, and inconsistent messages. First, like the employees in the last chapter whose boss failed to have the tough conversations with them, she spiritually quit. Her attitude shifted. She was unmotivated. She got by but she was not showing up. For two months she went through the motions.

The CEO noticed, of course—how could you not, when your star stops delivering results—but instead of asking what he might have done or what the company might have done to affect her results, he got annoyed. He asked her what *her* problem was. He never looked at the garbage he was slinging from his side of the street, and no matter how hard we asked him to look within and change his style, he simply demanded that she change and give the company her mindshare like before. He demanded that she come to work and do well and show up because "that was her job and she should act as motivated as she would if she worked at Google." That's when I finally opened my mouth.

"Whoa," I said. "Really? She should act as happy and as dedicated as if she works at Google but you have no duty to be or act like the Google managers who focus on that company's top three rules of train, mentor, and care? Tell me how that works."

Clearly, I was not long for that company, and neither was that star millennial. After I said my piece, she could not quit fast enough and the CEO could not fire her quick enough. All because the CEO refused to do the hard work to clean his side of the street first. In fact, he dismissed her as replaceable, and she may have been—but at what price? One that is too high and completely unproductive.

> What happens to you is because of you: Take personal responsibility and accountability to drive outcomes.

To avoid this and fully understand the power of cleaning your side of the street, follow these three steps to "Own It" in your role as a leader— for your own performance and in driving your team's results.

✓ **Operate from your foundation.** Individual strengths lead to team success; focus on them and use them to understand and leverage your team's strengths.

✓ **Choose your mindset.** Shift from an "excuses and losing" mentality to taking personal ownership for learning, solutions, your power, and your path.

✓ **Take personal accountability.** Ask what is your duty to yourself, your employees, and your company, and rate yourself on how well you do this.

If you've worked hard to bust the myths and become the real deal, these steps won't take too long to process, even if they take some time to really own.

Operate from Your Foundation

Cleaning your side of the street applies in even the most seemingly innocuous of situations, and even the most caring of leaders struggle with it. It is about a lack of self-awareness. Some leaders can be very giving of time but selfish in sharing themselves, and thus not connecting. They may help drive outcomes but they fail to allow millennials to drive the outcomes, as well. My clients who are truly open to coaching and mentoring (meaning they are coachable *and* they listen) get this, too—even when it comes to millennials. True leaders, whatever age or generation, grasp the fact that if they understand their own strengths, they can start to find help with their shortcomings—like a creative genius needing help with organization, or an engineer needing help with sales. They can learn to delegate, to share more. These leaders could then focus on what they are good at and shape the growth of their businesses by embracing differences and leveraging the strengths of others.

That's how we as a society can each take responsibility for the thrill, challenge, and opportunity, instead of the annoyance, when it comes to work with our millennials. Understanding your strengths and story allows you to do this and thus clean your side of the street. So why is it when we do work on strengths and story at launchbox, one of the biggest manager weaknesses is the inability to actually manage by delegating and using the strengths of their employees this way? Why is this so damned hard for most leaders to do?

In truth, most managers are self-taught, and they are scared of the loss of control that comes from motivating and creating results through others, so they refuse to do it. And when it comes to millennials, they are even more scared. I get it: Living inside those "walls" is really comfortable. To trust someone who works so completely differently than you do, is younger and less experienced, *and* questions you? Sounds real dangerous to me. Actually, it sounds like an excuse. As far as I can tell, non-millennials always feel like they will lose complete control when they have to trust millennials to do the work on their own. Managers like that are usually detail oriented and want to see the process. Just like we discussed in the second scene in "B: Bust Myths," they are worried their people won't do the work the way they would; they have absolutely no idea how to handle that and help the millennial through it, to guide but not control.

In situations like these, it may seem like managers are taking responsibility by doing it themselves to ensure proper completion. But all we are doing is fearing responsibility to avoid discomfort, which builds up resentment inside of our millennials and us. Because millennials want to do the work—remember, they value capability above all and want to learn and grow. We need to be strong enough to do this and get

> Stop being scared of coaching and being coached.

past our fear. If that CEO at the start of this chapter had been willing to clean his side of the street, he would have promoted that star employee and maybe even attracted three of her star friends to the company.

To get there takes us back to the foundational learning of Part One: You actually have to understand your own strengths to begin to connect with the world. Once you understand your own strengths and story, you unlock the power to see, interact with, connect to, and leverage your team's strengths and make a difference—which is exactly what that CEO failed to do with his star.

Think back now to Part One and be honest about what you're good at and what you're not good at. The same commitment you need to coach and mentor yourself is what you need to build a strong team of millennials. Be honest about what you can and can't do, and be willing to communicate and ask for help or delegate to others who are better at something—it's about leveraging your team. That's how you stand strong enough to choose the right mindset.

Choose Your Mindset

"Millennials really suck. I can't find a millennial who wants a job or who cares or shows up. They don't follow up and are not really interested in working all that hard," my friend said to me after one of our launchbox networking roundtables.

"Wait, *all* of them?" I asked.

"Well, not all of them; just the lazy ones. Most of them. Except my daughter. She's different. She and her classmates went to a great school and they have great jobs. They are tenacious. They are great. But the other ones really suck unlike any other group I've hired."

"Um, I'm not sure those millennials are statistically that different from other universities. Young is young. The difference is they are different. They all want to express some kind of individuality."

"But millennials just lack commitment. It's incredible."

"Have you tried to understand why you think this? Do you try and understand them before you judge?"

"Why?"

"Well, if millennials are different, then the facts have changed. Shouldn't we change our mind?"

"Why should I change?"

"Well, if what you are doing isn't getting you the results you want, what are you going to do differently in the face of all these horrible millennials?"

"I'm not sure you understand."

And . . . curtain.

Welcome to *The Blame Game*. The object of the game is to make everyone else the source of your problems: Mom blames Dad, daughter blames mother, teacher blames student, sales blames legal, accounting blames IT, distribution blames manufacturing . . . non-millennials blame millennials. The rules are simple, too: Shine the spotlight of blame on others, pointing out their deficiencies and problems, never shining it on yourself. Deny any hint that the problems might lie in *you*, that we are the source of all or most of our problems, not others.

There are no winners in the blame game, only losers, because what gets lost is any sense of personal responsibility and accountability to drive outcomes. The blame game ensures and assures that you never own your shit.

> Good relationships depend upon recognizing that we are the source of our problems.

The blame game is the worst game in the history of business. Stop playing it. *Now.*

As we learned in "B: Bust Myths," perceiving millennials as the source of our problems is traditional thinking that says they must change, not us. I can't understand this. If millennials offer something different than we do—something that connects them to tens of millions of potential customers and clients—why would we want them to change? Isn't this what we want in our business relationships? Shouldn't we understand the value of someone who offers different strengths than we do? If we have a weakness, doesn't it make sense to have an individual with that as one of their strengths?

Of course we get this. Except, it seems, when it comes to millennials. They "*suck*."

There is very little that can't be solved by taking initiative to do this daily. To get started, think back to a time you felt really frustrated or challenged when dealing with a millennial, or really anyone close to you—your significant other, your children, your mom—that ended with your thinking the other person was at fault. Write down what happened and how you reacted. Now take a step back and a deep breath and ask yourself these five questions without passing judgment on the other person.

1. Why was I frustrated?
2. Who was I blaming and why was I blaming them?
3. What could I have done to fix the situation or address the issue or challenge?
4. Who did I need to help me, based on my strengths and the strengths of others?

[Breathe deeply again]

5. How can I make solutions happen?

These questions effectively end blame, holding us accountable and responsible first for what we do in life and in business. Think back to my story in Part One. I had to learn how to be a parent and a spouse because I had few role models in my life. I had to learn how to find help through mentors, because no one was looking out for me. I had to learn to mentor myself by helping me control myself, and that meant holding myself responsible for everything I was doing and for the effects my actions had on others. That required both humility and for me to own my shit.

Getting past the blame game and deciding you're not going to blame millennials, or indeed anyone and everyone, for your problems is the essential first step in choosing your mindset. When it comes to owner-ship of your story and everything you do, choosing your mindset is first and foremost an act of self-accountability. Simply put, you can control only yourself in this world. And you have a duty to do so. Should you be honest about what you can do or not? Take ownership or not? Focus

on solutions or problems? These are the questions you confront when you choose your
mindset about what you want and whom you
serve. So ask yourself *"What can I do in every*

Who do you
control? You.

situation to make it better, change the focus, and drive the outcome?"

Listen, I am not telling you to give up all your power when choosing
your mindset. If you give it all away, how are you really being accountable? But you have to realize you can't completely control others. This
leader who fired all his millennials or the CEO who ignored his star
learned that the hard way. They effectively abdicated responsibility by
thinking they were controlling the situation by blaming millennials for
the problem, and not controlling themselves. That goes beyond failing to
assume positive intent (API) as we learned in "B: Bust Myths." That's an
inauthentic and toxic mindset stuck in the past.

What these leaders should have done was build relationships by
asking questions and connecting as the real deal. But authenticity gets
you only so far. You need to lead in a positive way, not just by API.

- thinking "learning opportunities" instead of "failures"
- thinking about what is learned or gained
- thinking about what can be done differently
- thinking of ways they can better support their team members
  next time

Thinking . . . and then *doing*. That's how you take personal ownership for learning and solutions. Doing anything else is to shift back to
excuses and a negative mentality. We can come up with every reason
that something did not happen. That's called making excuses. Excuses
are one of the few things that are simple *and* easy in this world, which is
why they are the sworn enemy of the hard work required to shift your
mindset to one of ownership, so you can be the boss you need to be.

Funny thing about that star millennial at the start of this chapter?
During her exit interview she told me she had screwed up, saw how she

quit too soon, and should have had a better attitude, but she was just frustrated and her boss would not communicate with her no matter how hard she tried. She owned her contribution. The CEO, on the other hand? He still isn't there. He still chooses this toxic mindset, burns through his employees, and remains unaware that he is responsible for cleaning his side of the street. He thinks everyone else should do it for him. Why? Because he is the CEO.

How is that working for him? How well are you handling these communication issues? Before you answer, remember the disconnects we discussed in the introduction: Millennials' frustrations with you are the same things you think you do well. Maybe you need to choose a mindset that starts by listening to them, and get to know your employees' names, brandstamps, and stories—and share yours! This is how we clean the street and take personal accountability.

Take Personal Accountability

What accountability structures do you have in place to make sure you are not the boss from above? Who or what is holding your people accountable to be their best selves? Who is holding you accountable? What do you use to measure your progress?

Reflecting on my story from Part One, for me it has been about finding the right mentors and advisory group to push me. It is about surrounding myself with people who say "no" and compel me to confront and overcome that "no" or listen to it when I am going off the rails. That's why I have a partner in my business who is the exact opposite of me—I need her to be my best self. If she does not say, "No, Dan!" or "That is not what you said or we discussed!" then who can?

That's my version of what Keith Ferrazzi—a terrific speaker, and author of two of my favorite books, *Never Eat Alone* and *Who's Got Your Back*—calls a "People Plan": pinpointing who can hold you accountable and help you achieve your goals. I have written my own People Plan and use it and the people who are part of it to constantly up my game and reshape what I know and who I am. That kind of plan requires real-deal relationships to work—relationships that force you to always consider what you think of yourself and what others think of your personal brand and how aligned they are (just like we covered in Part One). When you own it, you own both sides and they align.

But I want you to also consider another relationship here: the one to yourself. Ask yourself one question: What is the message you send to the world physically? I know that is a loaded question coming from me, considering my story: I am a cancer survivor. That survival led to a certain amount of vanity on my part. I have devoted myself to rigorous exercise and conscious eating to look and feel my best in everything I do.

I am especially conscious of my body language when I am communicating from the stage, participating in our launchbox programs, and interacting with my team and clients. This is not because I don't know that the seven-percent rule is a myth (that "communication is 93 percent nonverbal based on body language and tone of voice" is not true by any scientific standard) but because my personal brand depends on it. I know what I say means nothing if my body and mouth don't convey the same positive energy, emotions, and caring as my words. Nonverbals are all about emotions, which should rule our heads and hearts.

It wasn't until I was in my forties that I learned this completely—that I needed to be truly healthy of mind as well and take care of myself on a mental level by being my own mentor and holding myself accountable to this always. That's how I learned humility. That's when I started practicing mindfulness. Those who saw me as arrogant—and I can be arrogant sometimes—saw my arrogance in the service of them and accountable to something bigger than me.

That's what happened to my friend who after a decade running the high-tech company he founded thought he knew and had it all. He didn't need any help with accountability, because he was the guy with the gold and he created the rules. Thing is, my friend's rules *were* cool. People liked working for him. He was good to them and respected what they delivered. He didn't really need to learn B.R.I.D.G.E. as a management tool.

So why did he come to us at launchbox? Because he needed to learn to take care of and be accountable to himself. Sure, he had smartly enabled his team to take care of themselves by providing gym memberships, healthy snacks, and stress-reducing exercises. He thought he had done all he needed to do in his business to be mindful of and accountable to what his people—largely millennials—wanted and needed, and his relationships with them were solid as a result. But by never really participating in or finding similar tools for himself, he actually failed them by failing himself.

By not taking care of himself and being accountable to himself at the physical level, his endorphins weren't clicking. This is not some New Age mumbo jumbo; it is proven science: Exercising releases endorphins in the body, which interact with your brain to reduce your perception of pain and trigger positive feelings in your body. I have seen that reaction linked to feelings similar to when the body is given morphine. That's how powerful a "drug" exercising in even the smallest way can be.

> Take personal accountability for *yourself* first.

Without it, my friend just got more and more wound up and drenched in negativity—even while his business was doing well! He wasn't exercising. He was in terrible shape and eating poorly. And thus he started to fail. Not on the professional balance sheet, but the personal one. My friend's body and eventually his mind started to break down, jeopardizing his career.

When my friend showed up at launchbox, I felt for what he was going through on a personal and professional level. We had seen where breakdowns like his had led leaders, especially non-millennials, beyond poor physical health: alcoholism, drugs, prescription pill addiction, lost friendships, and domestic unrest. Their stories, like my friend's story—and mine before theirs—demonstrate the importance of one of our central launchbox philosophies: accountability to balancing mind/body/career.

By taking personal accountability and ownership for all three yourself, you get better at everything, because when you let in accountability personally, you create the space to figure out what's wrong in other areas. Because mind, body, and career are integrated. Without taking personal accountability for all three, one or more of them will begin to break down and not only affect the other two but every experience you have in the world. It will affect your clarity to drive success through better relationships—starting with the most important one: to yourself. Ownership of all three gives you clarity and insight into yourself and paves the way for progress in many areas—and happiness through better relationships, which, as we learned from Robert Waldinger's Harvard study in Part One, keep us happier and healthier.

As Waldinger revealed, good relationships protect our bodies and brains. So why are leaders—even successful ones like my friend—so hesitant to focus on the relationship with ourselves and see how this blocks us from owning the relationships with others and delivering real happiness? This is why choosing our mindset goes only so far. You can't just think about exercising and expect it to happen. You need to change your behavior, which is much, much harder. Balance in mind, body, and career is complicated and multifaceted, and choosing your mindset is only the first step. If you don't take accountability for changing the behavior that goes with that mindset, you will fail yourself and the people who connect to and depend on you.

Listen, I get it. The speed of business today makes it hard to slow down and assess accountability in this way, which is why we get annoyed with millennials who want to tune out or have that "me time" to create work/life balance. We never had that; why should they? Remember what I said in Part One about overwork and our inability to take vacations? Have I mentioned that Americans work the most hours of any industrialized nation in the world, save South Korea (where children get stressed out in an all-work-no-play education system) and Japan (where they have a word for dying at your desk: *karoshi*, or "death from overwork")? This is a powerful problem that can't be overcome by one vigorous workout at the gym. Great first step, but the real challenge is sustaining it. If you aren't into sports or don't have an elliptical machine gathering dust in a corner of your house, how about a walk at lunch or after you get home? Can't find physical release? How about just going into a room, closing the door, and having a good cry to let it all out? What works for you? Practice the Japanese art of *kaizen* or "continuous improvement," taking small steps, and let the people around you see how you keep it going, particularly your millennials who understand how important it is to take accountability to self.

Which is what my friend realized he needed to do. Once we showed him that he had failed to own his own wellness and to figuratively put on his own oxygen mask first, he began to breathe better by taking those steps to find balance. In turn, he took personal accountability in everything he did. His mind opened up. He had more clarity. He started to understand his journey on a deeper level and value himself as a way of delivering even more relevance to others than he ever had before. He felt more connected and engaged. He started to create other types of businesses. He got along better with his wife. And he had the best year he ever had in business. All because he understood that the message you send to the world physically is just as important in business as the culture you create. All because he held himself accountable to being a better, more mindful version of himself.

Millennials are a little better at understanding this connection between mind, body, and career than previous generations, and we could learn something from them in this regard. The future of accountability is here, and millennials have shown the way. Ironically, they also need help from us to hold them accountable.

Seeing and providing opportunities for wellness are not enough. You must compel yourself and your people to take advantage of those opportunities. You must make those opportunities part of the rules of engagement and values of your business. If your business wants to truly be accountable to your people, you can then integrate wellness into what you do, because accountability in the area of personal health and well-being—and indeed any area—can lead to breakthroughs and commitments to accountability in others.

That's what the first part of B.R.I.D.G.E. has been building toward: understanding, improving, taking care, and being accountable to yourself to be able to deliver value to others in all aspects of your life—professional *and* personal. Millennials want that. Invest in that passion and hold them accountable to it. That's an essential stake in maintaining the bridge over this gap. So hold up your end of the bargain by holding yourself accountable to your commitments. It is your job to set performance standards and hold everyone to those standards.

Ask yourself with your team, "Are we personally accountable?"

- Are we on the right track?
- Do we have the right people?
- Are we achieving our goals?
- Do I need to change anything?
- Am I in the way?

When personal and professional accountability are one and the same, modeling accountability from the top extends to much more than the work at hand. That's the experience I draw on to hold my team and myself accountable for what we do.

It's personal accountability at its most basic level: asking what is your fiduciary duty to yourself first, and then by extension to your team and your company.

To get there, I ask all of our clients this question, starting with the team and company: What is your duty to do a good job, to yourself and then to the organization, for taking the paycheck? It's great fun and extremely provocative to watch both millennials and non-millennials as they think about why they have this duty and what they owe their employer in the financial relationship, but then give themselves a free pass to ignore their fiduciary duty to the boss, business, customer, or anyone else, especially when that person is a pain in the ass. Millennials, as victims of parental coddling, are less likely to see this fiduciary duty to the company and boss right away. But when it comes to fiduciary duty to oneself, millennials and non-millennials both struggle as that starts with you and whether you actually think about having standards, a brand, and expectations, and want to be known for and as something.

And thus we have come full circle to the inside-out work we did in Part One: All of that work through to now has been for you to become other-directed and own the responsibility for building authentic relationships with your team. Now you move on to enabling your team to do the same to act and deliver value and results. If you can help them develop that skill, they will have an essential tool they can use and manifest for life. They're ready to own this and much more. That youthful perspective and ideation is contagious. Great things will come from showing them how to deliver value, have goals in mind, and empower their success.

MAKE IT HAPPEN:
I Control Myself and Live Accountability

Figuring out that I needed to get better, understand "me," and make a People Plan—to surround myself with others who were unafraid to push me and not just tell me how great my hair looks—has been essential to my living accountability. But as important was learning to clean my side of the street before asking others to clean theirs.

What can you do tomorrow to drive results for your manager, your team, and your company? How will you clean your side of the street? Great leaders must be personally responsible and accountable to drive the outcomes they want and need from others and themselves. Support your quest to make millennials own up to who they are by owning who you are.

1. **Operate from your foundation.** Individual strengths lead to team success; focus on them and use them to understand and leverage your team's strengths.
2. **Choose your mindset.** Get out of the blame game and turn the spotlight on yourself first when problems arise. Learn to see opportunity instead of annoyance when it comes to your millennials. Ditch the "excuses and losing" mentality to take personal ownership for learning and solutions.
3. **Take personal accountability.** Ask what is your duty to yourself, your employees, and your company. Hold *yourself* accountable to it all!

Remember: What happens to you is because of you. You control your mindset and thoughts. First ask yourself, *"Am I in sync with my strengths, skills, values, and passions?"* Then ask, "What can I do better to help?" Find your motivation: You have a duty and responsibility to reframe negative to positive—and always lead with a question.

D: Deliver Value

Serve and provide value to others every day.
Make it about them 24/7 and deliver
value through those relationships.

#movefrommetowe

In *Inferno*, Dante encounters this message as he passes through the gates of hell: "Abandon all hope, ye who enter here." I hope you have not abandoned hope, because we are halfway across this B.R.I.D.G.E.! You have had to abandon a lot of what you thought you knew in order to break through your assumptions about millennials, understand the power of authentic and caring relationships, and claim a keen sense of personal responsibility and accountability. Now I need you to abandon everything else you thought you knew in order to operationalize what we have covered.

Like Angry John, who we met at the start of Part One, I need you to abandon anything that remotely sounds like this: "When I was young, I walked two miles to the bus in the snow without shoes and never complained and so should they." First of all, that's just not true; you probably didn't do anything like that, and even if you did, you complained your ass off. Second of all, this is not about what happened to *you*; it is about what happens now and tomorrow, which is and will be completely different from when non-millennials grew up.

In other words, screw "the way it was." Just like I said about building relationships, it can't be about the past. This is the *new* normal in which the only way to make sure your people are contributing value on their own and as part of the whole is to get out of your own way and serve them. This not about "I"; this is about "we." This is about the value we provide to others. This is about answering one essential question.

How do you connect, mentor, lead, motivate, engage, and add value to those around you?

And what do leaders say the single biggest obstacle is to answering this question, making it about others, and managing their business and training their employees the right way to deliver value?

The big "why not" and "I can't because": Almighty Time.

Simply put, we live in a world of distraction—media and messages clamoring for our attention and all the data we need at our fingertips. Life today moves at a different speed than it did in the twentieth century—for *all of us*, not just millennials, though most of them have never known any other way of life.

- The typical office worker gets interrupted every eleven minutes and receives more than 100 emails a day.
- The average millennial gets more than 181 texts per day, up from 110 in 2011—and from how many when you started your career?
- The average millennial receives 100,000 words per day, an increase of 350 percent since 1980.

None of this is likely to get better in our lifetimes, so the only answer is to be more flexible, adaptable, and determined in dealing with the way things are.

Which is the main reason you need to abandon any notion of the way things were. You weren't interrupted every eleven minutes. Millennials have never known a world without mobile phones—shutting the door does not stop the words from coming in. Look at that data again. Do you really think that having to walk to the fax machine (remember those?) back in the day, you had it so bad? That millennials should operate the same way you did? Even if you think it is relevant, it is not the same.

> What can you do tomorrow to provide more value to others?

I'm not saying time isn't a huge obstacle to delivering value. It simply cannot be an excuse for not making it about others—to providing value and projecting that value internally through the company and externally to your partners and customers to deliver what they need.

So how do you shift your mindset and maximize the time you have to serve and provide value in the workplace and marketplace?

✓ **Be the right kind of giver.**
✓ **Shift to mentor.**
✓ **Make it about others.**

Be a Giver

Andrea, a young millennial professional I was working with, came to me with a quandary: She wanted to add more value at her company, but she needed more engagement and responsibility from her bosses to do so. As the youngest and newest member of the team, there was only so much she could contribute on her own initiative. She felt marginalized and disengaged as her bosses ran around, busy with the work at hand.

This was hard for Andrea to tell me, because she didn't want to sound negative about the company. She had joined the company because she respected the people and the work they did and had done. She still did. She was proud to tell her friends and anyone she met about the people she worked for. She was "all in." She showed up prepared to work hard every day and do "whatever it takes." She had tried to be a self-starter and proactive in her own development, asking the partners the details of what they needed, what they needed from her, and how she could assist them in achieving results. But she was struggling with her role among them and her place at the company on a day-to-day basis.

Andrea's story resonated with me, because she did *not* blame her bosses for this. She was talking to me because *she* needed to figure out how better to talk to *them*. She was scared about saying the wrong thing, though, which was the last thing she wanted. Andrea said the few times they had engaged her had been challenging and exhilarating. "But it is hard to keep asking, 'What else can I do?' and hear, 'Nothing right now,' 'I'll get back to you,' 'Let me ask around,' or worse, no response at all."

I felt for Andrea. She didn't feel entitled. She didn't feel angry. She simply felt disappointed that she delivered no value and had no idea how to add the value she felt she could give.

The thing is, Andrea wasn't ever going to get to deliver that value unless her bosses became givers.

In his best-selling book, *Give and Take,* Wharton School professor Adam Grant divides us into three kinds of people: givers, takers, and matchers. Of course, everyone is a mixture of all three types, but one is usually dominant. The question is what type are you and what type do you need to be to deliver value? Grant offers a free "Giver/Taker/ Matcher Assessment" on his website (*http://bit.ly/1kOS4Rg*), but the types break down like this.

- Takers have one simple modus operandi: get as much as possible from others.

- Matchers hate takers and actually make it their mission to take the takers down; they believe what goes around should come around—quid pro quo, baby!—and aim to trade evenly.
- Givers are the opposite of takers, and unlike matchers, they give something without expecting or taking something in return.

And who does Grant say are the highest performers and most successful in life? The givers. Why? Actually Grant's thinking has evolved a bit in that regard since his book was published. As he noted in an article for *The Atlantic* in 2014, "When I wrote the book, I attributed the long-term success of givers to two major forces: relationships and motivation. From a relationship perspective, givers build deeper and broader connections . . . From a motivation perspective, helping others enriches the meaning and purpose of our own lives, showing us that our contributions matter and energizing us to work harder, longer, and smarter." But then Grant added a third reason: learning. Learning builds knowledge and facilitates giving—the old adage that you get back what you give.

The bad news is that being a giver is probably not the way many non-millennials were taught as the path to their success. The good news is that through the inside-out work you did in Part One and all the B.R.I.D.G.E. work so far, the answers should not be too hard to find. Even if you are a taker or a matcher, you are well prepared to become better givers through learning,

> To deliver value and enable it in others, shift to "Giver Leadership."

having relationships with, and helping *anyone*, but most directly for the purpose of this book: millennials—be they givers like Andrea, takers, or matchers.

What does this mean? It means shifting to "Giver Leadership"—being a giving leader who delivers value by asking

- How does my role add value in the workplace, especially to others?
- How do I deliver value internally to my employees and externally to my partners and customers every day?
- How many "I's" do I use as opposed to "we's" in my emails, workplace correspondence, and presentations? Is it about us or me?

That's how Giver Leadership shifts your mindset from "me" to "we." That's how a giving leader adds value to others by collaborating with and supporting team members and clients to help them be successful. That's how giving leaders create authentic and caring relationships to build connections the right way. That's all Andrea, most millennials, and indeed most people today need to start delivering value back: to feel a part of something.

But you didn't think it was that simple, did you? Of course not. So here's the rub: According to Grant, givers are not only the highest performers and most successful in life but also the *lowest* performers and *least* successful in life. That's right, givers are overrepresented at both extremes. Grant writes, "[Givers who enjoy] helping others can be inefficient in the short run but surprisingly productive in the long run. Givers tend to start out with lower sales revenue and lower medical school grades. In sales, givers often put their customers' needs above their own sales targets. In medicine, before big exams, givers are so busy helping their friends study that they fail to fill the holes in their own understanding. Yet after a year in sales, the highest revenue belongs to those same generous people, and by the end of medical school, the top grades belong to the students with the most passion for helping others."

The same is true of Giver Leadership.

So how do you go from a giving leader whose generous spirit sinks you, to a giving leader who swims? This is no easy task. Grant has written extensively on the topic, including an essay for the *Harvard Business*

Review in which he said, "This creates a challenge for managers. Can they promote generosity without cutting into productivity and undermining fairness? How can they avoid creating situations where already-generous people give away too much of their attention while selfish coworkers feel they have even more license to take? How, in short, can they protect good people from being treated like doormats? Givers need to distinguish generosity from three other attributes—timidity, availability, and empathy. Part of the solution must involve targeting the takers in the organization—providing incentives for them to collaborate and establishing repercussions for refusing reasonable requests. But even more important, my research suggests, is helping the givers act on their generous impulses more productively."

And that brings us back to the biggest obstacle in delivering value: Time.

Giver Leadership gets crushed by time—or rather, the lack of it crushes those potentially amazing Giver Leaders. Consider what one of my leadership clients told me: "I'm always late. I want to be a leader, but I just have too many demands. Everyone gets in the way of me being on time and having time and prioritizing. There are too many distractions."

Understand this client was a successful "grown ass" man telling me that "everyone" put so much stuff on his plate that he was late all the time. I confronted him in a way that will feel familiar after the previous chapter.

"Really?" I said. "'They' make you out of control? *They* put all this stuff on you and force you to take it on, and as a result you can't prioritize your time well enough so you have trouble being on time? *You* don't need to make it happen? Think about the message that sends to your team, your company, and your clients."

As I am wont to do with my clients, I didn't stop there. I went through all the accountability issues we covered in "I Own It": He needed to own his problem; he, not "them," had allowed himself to get out of control; he needed to move away from the blame game and make things happen . . . Then I realized my client had a problem beyond responsibility and accountability. There was something really good about what he was doing. He cared and was giving of his time; he was trying to be a giving leader. But that was the problem—all that giving was killing him.

Giver Leadership is essential to delivering value to others, but only when you give productively and don't let the takers take.

What's the solution? One way is to limit your time to help, and when that time is gone, it is gone. And stop doing things just because you feel you must. Sympathy and empathy are wonderful traits but they will eat you up and distract you from less emotionally charged but important work. You can't fix everyone and you shouldn't try. (I want you to care, but overcaring is just as bad for you as being care-less.)

But I believe the best way to be the right kind of giver is to be an assertive giver and lead from your strengths. Really understand how you "value up" using Giver Leadership. Start by reviewing your strength and skills (especially the WIFThem practice) from Part One. Then look at how Giver Leadership can use those strengths and skills to create real impact for internal and external customers.

Here is how I find out how to articulate my strengths and skills to "value up" and provide kick-ass help to those customers (be they employees, external partners, clients and customers, or even family and friends): I use my gift for asking questions. First, I ask permission to help and give advice because without permission I can just go home—few, if any, will listen to what I have to say. Then, I move into issue recognition. I start by trying to understand what the person needs from me by asking him or her questions.

- What is the issue?
- What are you trying to accomplish?
- What is the result you are looking for?
- What can we accomplish relative to your goal now?
- How can I help?

When I get the answers, I ask even more questions to make sure I understand as many facts as possible (objective and subjective). I want to best figure out what the person needs from me in the moment and moving forward to get the results that will set him or her free from the issue. Is it listening? Action? "Carefrontation coaching?" Advice? Help framing a conversation or presentation, referring a resource, or resolving conflict? I use the question-asking skills from the "Real Deal" chapter to provide a solution that truly is about the other person and delivers value to him or her. And when I am done, I ask even more questions to understand how to better deliver value in the future: Did what I deliver help? Did you get what you needed or wanted? Can I can do anything else or help you find someone who can?

This is how I deliver value and embrace Giver Leadership. What are you going to do? Know your strengths and skills and connect them to Giver Leadership. That's how you become your strongest, most assertive self and use that giving as connection currency, to help and learn in the best ways possible. This is what Andrea needed to do to assert herself and be clear on what she needed to help deliver her value. Strikingly, it also engaged her bosses and compelled them to reciprocate, providing her with value and time, and in turn, maximizing her value.

This is what another client of mine, Margot, did to show value in the work she did. Margot is a lawyer at a major law firm where ego is never a bad word. She was petrified to speak in public and tell her story in no small part because she felt what she had to say was irrelevant. With that came low self-esteem that diminished the power of her biggest strengths: helping others, creating harmony, showing empathy, and taking responsibility for making sure everyone was okay. In other words, she just worked quietly on the sidelines rather than speaking out publicly and assertively, never giving herself credit for how special a giver she was. She was always harmonizing everyone else without taking care of what she needed. Basically, she blended into the wall.

When Margot learned about how her strengths actually created a duty for her to be more proactive in helping others it was an *aha* moment. She worked through her fear of storytelling and realized she had a position that commanded attention and a story that could help others. Her

Giver Leadership immediately became more assertive, as did her sense of self-worth and confidence to help herself *before* she helped others.

In other words, she put on her value "oxygen mask" first before helping others affix theirs. Her ownership of the value in her strengths turned her into a giver who swims rather than sinks. She soon showed the partnership at the firm that being a giver could not only deliver value but also show others the way by becoming a mentor to the younger millennial lawyers.

Shift to Mentor

In the "Recognize Your Skills, Passions & Values" chapter of Part One, I told the story of how I went from a high-tech Silicon Valley start-up to a low-tech auto business and wound up having a great learning experience. I didn't know anything about the business when they hired me and they knew it. But what did one of the partners say to me?

"Dan, you don't need to know anything," he said in his deep drawl. "I'm gonna teach you everything you need to know here. You're a smart guy. I'll teach ya everything."

And that's what he did. He may have been crazy, but he was my kind of crazy and an amazing mentor. Not a manager—a real mentor who at the beginning coached me to see how my strengths and story delivered value to him and the company. *This is your duty to your millennial workforce.*

I know I am not the first person to talk about the importance of mentoring and the shift from managing to coaching in the workplace. Over time, we have shifted from trainers to supervisors to managers and now to coaches and mentors. Think of leaders who coach as the best version of those you see on the sidelines of every sport. They are much more involved and employee- and team-focused than managers. And mentors? They aren't just people who you meet

> You have a duty to coach, teach, and mentor— to help next-generation leaders learn and grow.

with twice a year for sage advice; they are the people who have your back and are vested in your success. Teachers, coaches, and mentors— these are people your millennials and we want leaders to be all at once. This shift in expectation has never been more important than when dealing with the millennial generation. A company that cares about career development through mentoring and coaching is much more apt to get millennials to want to do things for it, and earn more loyalty from all its employees—even if those employees leave. Because people will leave.

Unless they leave for illegal, discriminatory, or malicious reasons, every millennial who leaves your company must be a great cheerleader for your business and leadership and should be able to refer you employees and business. So while you have them, take the time to mentor and coach them—and they just might stay. If mentoring seems super needy to you—a real pain in the ass—consider this: In a Sun Microsystems mentoring program, participants who were mentees, not surprisingly, had a retention rate 23 percent higher than nonparticipants. More surprisingly, those who leaned in as mentors had a retention rate 20 percent higher than nonparticipants, saving Sun an estimated $6.7 million. Sun also found that mentoring programs increased the level of trust in organizational leadership across the entire company.

Still think mentoring has no impact on retention or ROI?

Yes, even with mentoring, millennials will fail. So what? Let them. The important thing is that you understand—fail or succeed or anywhere in between—that *for millennials, experience equals value and mentoring gives them that experience.* That is what they want: capability, not employability. As one millennial explained it

We respond to the culture of the organization, but we need a trusting relationship from day one to guide us and mentor us. We want to understand what we are doing, not just be told to do it. We want to experience and see it all. We value and need that caring and nurturing and expect it. But we respond to it with results.

Ask yourself: How are you delivering that value? What experiences are they getting from you? How are you using your strengths to teach and share the knowledge you have? When was the last time you gave one of them the opportunity to learn how to do your job and see you in action?

- **Mentors teach** from experience and learn together with their people, sharing insights; bosses just assign work.
- **Mentors model the way** by providing opportunities for employees to observe and learn from them in different situations; bosses just tell them what to do.
- **Mentors lead individually**, working one-on-one and checking in regularly; bosses just manage groups.
- **Mentors work for development**, planning activities and solving problems together; bosses just work to get things done.
- **Mentors care more**; they define themselves as what they do for the people who work for them and measure themselves accordingly.

Let me be clear again on one thing: Mentoring comes naturally to givers. As a result, to do it in the most productive way, you must not only take those steps but also avoid the traps givers fall into: Invest time and be flexible when you can, but limit it; just focus completely when you do, making mentoring about quality, not quantity. Don't overcare and let empathy rule the mentoring roost. And be assertive!

Yes, you can overmentor and coach. You have the millennial who keeps changing his or her mind and one day wants to do sales and when that gets too tough suddenly wants to be a project manager? What's next, being an engineer? Millennials can be very headstrong on what they want to do and when they want it; they expected their parents would cure their problem and help them do it. As I said in the opening of the book, we love *and* hate this, so we must encourage it to a point and then resist it.

Enabling change is important to evolution, but enabling constant change makes you less and less valuable to millennials and them less valuable to you. Mentoring must have some hard lines, too. Millennials must have responsibility in the mentoring relationship, too, and not only to show up and open up but also to "reverse mentor" and be givers as well—be the teachers to their learning non-millennial managers to deliver value back to them and be productive and effective team members. In other words, they must own the relationship and take responsibility for their progress and development. They have different knowledge and experience and must share that. They know the problems, so they should help shape the solutions. They know you have a schedule; they need to respect that and be available and prepared always.

> Push and pull together to connect and challenge yourself and your millennials to create and innovate.

To get anywhere, mentoring requires a lot of push and pull on both sides, not simply pushing or pulling at the same time. Without that mutuality, mentoring becomes like that strange creature from Dr. Doolittle, the pushmi-pullyu (pronounced "push-me-pull-you")—a creature that has two heads at opposite ends of its body. Problem was, when one head pushed, the other pushed, too. When one head pulled, the other did the same. As a result, the creature rarely went anywhere and most of the time stood still.

That's a surefire recipe for disaster in business: doing nothing.

Because nothing has no value and adds no value to your millennials, which is what happened with Andrea at the start of the chapter when her partners never pushed or pulled her.

Get your people out of their comfort zone and *push* them to use their strengths to deliver value by

- creating stretch opportunities for employees to learn, grow, and maybe even fail
- collaborating, questioning, engaging, ideating
- encouraging employees to "lean in"

And then *pull* by

- building an environment that encourages questioning the status quo, identifying new solutions, and allowing time for the creative flow of ideas
- being willing to encourage entrepreneurship through experimenting and exploring those ideas
- rewarding curiosity and informed risk taking—accepting and redirecting failure

But don't forget: You can give millennials these push–pull opportunities and the mentoring and teaching time and resources to make it happen, but they have to want it and push and pull back. They can't just expect stretch goals. They must *ask* for them and then deliver on them. They can't just expect success and get a trophy for participation like they did playing sports growing up; they must take responsibility for and own successes and failures. They must overdeliver and ask what more can they do to help you and the company be successful. Millennials cannot question the status quo on their own terms—that violates most conditions of employment. They simply must align their actions with shared values through the dance of push and pull that your mentoring facilitates.

> Find balance between pushing and pulling to deliver value to your millennials and have them deliver better value to you.

I'll never forget the night I attended a crowded legal networking event and spotted a woman who had come through our B.R.I.D.G.E. program. We had just coached her on how to network and I was eager to see what she had absorbed. But that was impossible. I never saw her alone; she and two other associates moved around the room in a pack.

I found one of the non-millennial partners, pointed out what I saw, and asked why. "Well," he said, "I tell them to go around in groups so they don't feel awkward." I was so stunned I must have paused ten seconds before I found my words—a near record for me in these situations. I mean, these were big law firm associates making $150,000-plus a year and billing at hundreds of dollars an hour—and this partner did not think he could tell them when they go to a networking event to try and talk to people on their own to build business? That they should have to hold someone's hand? *Really?*

And you wonder why we complain about millennials. We haven't taught them anything and too often we don't demand anything of them. So demand it.

Remember from our strengths work in Part One: The goal is to have you and your team kick ass. Everywhere they and you wish. More and more. You are looking to teach and help millennials learn to do this and you're also looking for teaching and learning *from* them. Don't fall into the trap of that partner at the networking event. He may have thought he was acting in the interests of his associates, but he was not mentoring them—he never pushed them to kick ass for him.

He had shifted back to "me" from "we"—something that is too easy for us to do.

Make It About Others

At a bar mitzvah, I found myself reconnecting around the table with some old friends who hadn't seen me in decades. "I hear you've been with your wife for thirty years and yet you look so young and great," one of my old friends said. "I heard you are so happy. How'd you do it? What's the secret to such a long-lasting relationship?"

I smiled. "Some years ago, I learned to stop sucking every bit of air out of the room and it worked."

All the women at the table looked at each other and then at their husbands with a silent chorus of *Did you hear what he just said?* and *That's what you do.* So do most of us. Not just husbands or men; wives and women are just as guilty, especially in the workplace. All because we fail to observe one important rule: *You are not the hero of your story.*

> Your audience—
> your employees and
> your customers—
> must be the heroes
> of your story.

Who is the hero of your and your company's story? *Your audience.* If you want to create results and have an impact on employees and customers, you need to deliver value to them every day. Creating a system that communicates, adds, and delivers that value in the workplace and marketplace starts with making sure you remember to make it about "them"—make others the heroes of your stories, not you. In other words, we need to actively fight our instincts to suck the air out of the room, and instead employ Giver Leadership and make our stories about the receiver and what we can do for them.

Here's what I mean by that. Think of how much you loathe listening to a boasting, overinflated, me-centric, often bloviating family member, colleague, or dinner party guest. (Not a talk radio host or keynote speaker at a convention of like minds: They are paid to be exactly this way and to entertain while doing it.) The kind of person who, when he or she is done talking, says, "Okay, I am done talking about me. Now can you tell me a story that talks about me?"

I have a relative like this. I am not sure she ever gets down to understanding that it is about others although she holds herself up as the everyman who talks to everyone and is so fantastic. The problem isn't that she is lying. The problem is that it's done with a ton of attention to how great she is at doing that. She is the hero of all conversations. Even when she tells you about what she learned from someone, it is about how special she is that she learned it. I am not saying she is a bad person. She is even entertaining. But that entertainment will never be about you. It is a one-way street. That's not caring; that's neglect.

Why do you think this person and people like her can't see how she is? Has anyone told her this is how she is perceived? Likely not, even if we could get a word in edgewise. Because *we* don't exist independently of her. And here is the rub: She has been really successful for most of her career in large companies. But she has a terrible track record of leading, retaining, and mentoring her people—and that has started to cost her in the age of the millennial. The question is: *Will she understand why it's costing her before it is too late?* Not if she fails to see value in deeper connections.

Of course, my family member is an extreme example, but not that extreme. Our normal, self-centered ways have everything to do with the lack of trust that has built up in business and undermined our connections to our people— millennial and beyond. How do you teach millennials to understand their value, share why it matters to others, and deliver value that becomes results? It starts from within: Show *them* how *you* deliver value each and every day. Project it. Do it. *Be it.*

> Your story is about the audience, not you—or rather, the audience *through* you.

Delivering value is about action—it's about you completing a project on time, solving a problem, learning a new skill, and more. It's not just talking; it's about communicating and then showing how you can do, help, go above and beyond, and deliver value to others. Sounds easy, but I never saw a more powerful example of how hard it can be to communicate value than when I worked with some real heroes.

As part of my being a Giver Leader, I work at The Honor Foundation, where we help Navy SEALs and other special operatives go from deployment to employment. We help them understand their strengths, skills, values, and passions. We work on the power of questions. We then have them do their three-minute story pitch. And like every other group, they completely tank. Every. Time. Why? Because they have been taught and trained in humility—not humblebragging but real humility: It's about the mission, not the individual; trust in the collective and put the team first.

Most SEALs have a hard time even saying they were in the SEAL program. They don't like to say how special they are. As a result, it is hard for them to see how their skills in the armed forces translate to civilian life where they need to articulate what those skills and experiences are so that potential employers know how good they would be at doing a job.

These SEALs have managed hundreds of people in strategic and complicated operations, been responsible for millions upon millions of dollars of equipment and lives, and made quick decisions in the most stressful of situations on a level few will ever understand. Who wouldn't want that kind of person on a team? Yet the SEALs struggle to see it. Despite being nothing but other-directed in their military careers, they have a difficult time translating all their strengths and skills and articulating their value in a story. Because they have not figured out that the value of articulating their story is not about them. It is about how they can help the listener by being themselves, and describing themselves in ways that make meaningful connections so they can provide their value in the commercial world.

Which makes the Navy SEALs ironic and extreme examples of most millennials and managers I work with. Their seemingly surprising inability to be clear on communicating their value shows just how this can be a critical deficit. I have never met men more intensely capable and qualified, not to mention conditioned to make it about others at every turn.

The SEALs lived by delivering value in everything they do yet they have a hard time communicating that value. My duty to them is the same duty we have to our teams, our companies, and our customers and clients: help them understand and communicate how they deliver value. It is up to me as their giving leader to show them how to overcome their conditioning and mindset and learn to show how they can deliver value on a different "battlefield."

Making it about others means getting rid of your ego and giving to others—not to coddle and be overgenerous to a fault, but to add value as it relates to the strategic vision and what the organization wants and needs in terms of results. These are the principles we must learn to use to thrive in our personal and professional lives. These are the principles we teach the SEALs and other Honor Foundation Fellows as they learn to exercise the muscle of articulating real value to others when their call of duty ends. To do this they need to feel what they probably never did alone on the battlefield: safe. They need to know that we have their backs.

Do you have the backs of your employees? Are you creating a safe and engaged workplace where people feel good and continue to grow? Our duty to our people in the workplace should be the same as a parent to a child: To teach them to be the best person that they can be—improve them; improve their home and business lives. Do that and I guarantee they will be much more apt to do more for us and focus on how they are delivering value in return.

MAKE IT HAPPEN:
Deliver on Value Through Giver Leadership, Mentorship, and Making It About Others

It took me until I was in my forties to realize that making what you do about others is the greatest tool for success. Whether I was in the law, sales, or career development, or simply honing my personal and professional relationships, nothing has worked better. It is how we started launchbox. What you give *always* comes back to you in some way if you give to others the right way.

What are you doing to be relevant and provide more value to others? How can you serve and provide value to your employees and company every day? How can you mentor them to do the same for you, each other, and clients/customers? Use your strengths, values, skills, passions, and stories to make it about others. Find the time and overcome your allegiance to the way things have always been and do these three things daily.

1. **Be the right kind of giver.** Move from "me" to "we" and embrace Giver Leadership in everything you say and do—really believe it all comes back in the end. But do it the right way. Be focused, caring but not empathetic, and assertive, to control the takers and enable more giving.

2. **Shift to mentor.** You are a teacher and a role model. Take the time and make the investment in sharing your knowledge and experience to help your employees get better and to provide opportunities for employees to observe and learn from you—and expect something back from them. Create an environment that encourages questioning and pushes people (including yourself) beyond their comfort zones.

3. **Make it about others.** Remember, you are not the hero of your own story. Get rid of your ego and be truly other-directed!

G: Goals in Mind

Create alignment around shared goals and
priorities to increase engagement and trust.

#purpose #transparency

Here's a lesson from Mom that is still (mostly) true in life: Breakfast is the
most important meal of the day. Here's a lesson from Andrew Carnegie
that is still (mostly) true in business: "If you want to be happy, set a goal
that commands your thoughts, liberates your energy, and inspires your
hopes." What's also (mostly) true about both these things? Too many of
us skip over their importance.

I am not saying that you don't know that goals, like breakfast, are
important. I have never worked with a client who did not have goals or
at least acknowledge their importance. Goals describe what a company
expects to accomplish to reach its objectives with measurable results
over a specific period of time. Not many companies survive without
some sense of that. What I am saying is: Knowing something is important and actually making it important are two different things. Like so

many others factors in life, the bustle and distractions that start the moment we wake up too often push things like breakfast and goals to the proverbial back burner. They may always "be there"—you probably have cereal, oatmeal, yogurt, or something for breakfast in the kitchen and goals and objectives listed in your company's business plans and annual reports. But did you check the expiration date on that yogurt? It's probably as dated as the goals in those plans and reports. Outta sight, outta mind.

And here's something else that's (mostly) true about breakfast and goals: The longer we ignore them, the more likely we are to rush to address that ignorance in the wrong way. The most unhealthy breakfast meals are consumed on the run. The most thoughtless, misguided, and disconnected goals are created in an act of disingenuous annual compliance at the eleventh hour.

Wake up!

That donut you scarfed in a hurry is not good for your body, and that approach to goals is not only dated but also shows a complete lack of caring that is beyond bad for your millennials and your business as a whole. If you care so little about the company's goals that you pay only token annual homage to them, why should millennials or any employee care more than that?

I once had a boss who wrote down his goals for the year on a piece of paper the size of a Post-it and carried it around in his wallet all year long. Every time he opened his wallet, he saw those goals. They were with him always until the end of the year when he pulled out the paper and assessed them. He cared that much. But even that closeness only gets you so far, because you need to care about the goals of the people who work for you, too. In other words, when it comes to goals, waking up only solves part of the problem. You can find the source of that problem in one word that appears three times in Andrew Carnegie's otherwise excellent quote: "your."

This is not just about you.

How do you create meaningful goals that will command the thoughts, energy, and commitment of your millennials?

✓ **Have a shared vision and shared goals** that create alignment between individuals, the team, and the company.

✓ **Lead with transparency and purpose** to increase engagement and trust.

✓ **Measure to create results.** Have metrics for progress toward goals, and plow achievements into new collaborations, innovations, and plans to maintain them.

Have a Shared Vision and Shared Goals

Here's a conversation I had with a client in the hospitality industry.

"Millennials are horrible. All they want to do is surf and text all day. They don't want to go to work," he said.

"Well, you must be complicit in some way." I said.

"What do you mean? What do I have to do with them surfing?"

"Are you a teacher? Are you a mentor? How good a manager are you? Do you ask them what they think or why they surf? They may want to surf during the day when it is sunny and then work all night for you to get the work done. Do you accept that? Do you have a plan for that?"

"That's just ridiculous. Why don't they just come to work and work?"

"Well, that's a pretty old framework for success."

"I don't care. I just fire the millennials."

"And how's that working for you?"

"Fine."

"Fine? Okay, is that expensive, to continually hire people? Does it feel good to repeatedly have to train new people? Do you feel good about the way you are dealing with your millennials?"

Silence.

"Did you ever consider that they may just have goals that don't align with yours and your goals don't align with what they are actually doing?"

"I don't care."

I have had similar conversations with dozens of clients. "We want to promote from within," the clients say, "but millennials don't want to stick around. They have such a sense of entitlement." In the "B: Bust Myths" chapter, we discussed how to assume positive intent around assumptions of entitlement, and here's another layer: *What you see as entitlement is often an expression of a powerful need to pursue individual goals, not just the goals of the company.*

You must find a way to embrace those individual goals as part of the shared vision for the company. To dismiss them as just entitlement or with an "I don't care" attitude is to dismiss how millennials find purpose and relevance and make you irrelevant to them. It will not only drive them away but also deprive you of the power you can create through shared visions and goals.

Consider what this millennial told an audience of business leaders at launchbox.

> Yes, all the things they say about millennials apply to me. I am ADD. I am purposeful. I want things to have meaning so I search for it constantly. You think we don't want to do the work like you did and that is true—we don't. But that does not make me lazy. I want to work. I am just forward thinking and don't want to compromise who I am, so I took responsibility for that. When I was looking, I knew I wanted to be in business development or sales so I went to the local business journal to look for the businesses that met my professional criteria and my personal criteria, like having volunteering be part of the job.

Simply put, *shared goals create a shared purpose.* We have an obligation to share and care about people and their individual goals. To move from "me" to "we" when it comes to goals, we must make our millennials' (and all of our employees') goals a central part of how we engage them and show that we care. This is about *them*—where they are going, not just what they are doing. That goes beyond understanding why you are doing something in the workplace. It ties to something we discussed in the introduction: what Simon Sinek, in *Start with Why: How Great Leaders Inspire Everyone to Take Action*, calls your "why" or the purpose, cause, or

> Individual goals and company goals and visions must be aligned and shared.

belief that inspires you to do what you do and makes you passionate about working.

Leaders must see not only the importance in living and sharing this why through their and the company's goals, but also the value in their employees' and customers' individual whys—and authentically care about them. Without that caring, leaders and their companies can't expect their goals to be shared by millennials and by extension have their millennial customers buy into them.

For example, it is great for a business like Umpqua Bank, which has more than 300 branches in the western United States, to redefine itself around customer service and community, tailoring its branches to fit the lifestyle of its customers, particularly millennials. One branch in a young family-oriented area welcomes kids inside and often breaks out a free ice cream truck. But if the employees don't share the goal to provide that service and connect it to what they are doing, then service and communication will suffer. That's not something a free Popsicle can cure. Umpqua seems to understand this. According to *Consumer Reports*, Umpqua puts your money where its mouth is: It does have highly rated customer service and communication.

Is it so foreign to us to help our people engage their personal and professional ambitions through the work they do for us? The old-school management style and belief that you are either with us or against us just does not apply anymore. Millennials must feel and be responsible for their career plans and goals, but still we must guide them. They need us and we need them. Remember, your goal is to guide millennials, yet allow them the power to figure it out and be innovative and creative in creating that shared purpose. (Apply your ability to WIFThem from the "Skills, Passions & Values" chapter here.)

If we live Giver Leadership like we learned in "D: Deliver Value" and give the right way when it comes to valuing everyone's goals, then this good comes back to us in the end in a big way. Everyone is all in and aligned around BIG GOALS that support that shared purpose and the goals of the company.

Big goals equal best outcomes. Setting goals increases performance and productivity 11 to 25 percent. That's like adding two extra hours of work every day just by building a mental framework around the activity. But only if you keep the goals aligned with individual purpose. As Edwin Locke and Gary Latham wrote in "New Directions in Goal-Setting Theory" (*Current Directions in Psychological Science*, 2006), "Big goals work best when there's an alignment between an individual's values and the desired outcome."

Ask yourself these questions.

- Do you define and share goals and strategy to create alignment and trust?
- Do you know how goals tie into individual strengths and responsibilities and core values that create a meaningful shared purpose?
- Do your millennials know, understand, and contribute to the company's strategy and goals and the results needed/required?
- Does everyone understand their role in achieving the goals?
- What can you do tomorrow to create alignment around shared goals between the company, the team, and individuals?

These are difficult questions to answer, and most companies and leaders we work with don't have clear answers. So we use an exercise called "Connect the Dots," which we recommend doing regularly.

EXERCISE:

Connect the Dots

1. Take the company's top five goals and priorities and write each one in big letters at the top of five large sheets of easel paper or in five columns on a large whiteboard.
2. Ask every team member or employee to think about what they do in their jobs and list the top five things on Post-its and sign their names.
3. Have everyone stick the Post-its directly under the company goal it most appropriately aligns with. Have them hold on to any Post-it that does not fit.
4. Don't discuss anything yet. Have everyone sit back down and write the answer to the following question on another Post-it—preferably a different color Post-it: Where is an area or what is something you would like to or could do to support one of the company's goals?
5. Have everyone sign that Post-it and stick it under the company goal it most appropriately aligns with.
6. Do a "gallery walk" as a group through all the goals and the Post-its under them.
7. Discuss:
   • Where are areas of alignment?
   • Where are there areas of misalignment? (Look at the Post-its still in people's hands, and the goals that have few or no Post-its under them.)
   • Where are areas of opportunity?

The first goal of the "Connect the Dots" exercise is to answer the question: *How does what I do help achieve the company's goals? Why am I important to the company?*

Answering these questions compels each person to see on their own and as a group how their individual responsibilities connect to, support, and align with the goals of the company and where they do not so that disconnects can be addressed. Go ahead and celebrate the alignments, but if your people are doing a bunch of things that don't support the goals of the company, then you better come together after the exercise to create new priorities for them that *are* aligned—before they start looking for a new job. Or you need to create new goals for the company that actually align with the work being done.

The second goal of the "Connect the Dots" exercise is to answer the question: *What would I like to do that I could do but am not doing to support the goals of the company?* Answering this question allows leaders to see the opportunities to engage and get more value by leveraging strengths, skills, or passions of their people to achieve the goals of the individual and the company. When the dots are connected, you align and create shared purpose around individual, team, and company goals and lay the foundation for clear expectations, roles, and direction for achieving them.

Now, how about changing how you think about the goals themselves? How about we move from SMART goals to *meaningful* goals?

At one point or another in your professional career, you probably encountered SMART goals, namely goals that are Specific, Measurable, Attainable, Realistic, and Timely. You might even use them or some version of them yourself, and that's fine . . . for 1981. Which is when SMART goals were created. Before Apple had a Mac, before the Internet, before the Berlin Wall fell. We can and must do better than that in the millennial age to knock down the walls between our goals and our millennials' goals. This is a generation that wants more. They don't just want shared purpose; they want shared meaning.

> Move from SMART goals to meaningful goals to increase engagement and trust among your employees and your clients.

I first heard the idea of meaningful goals from my friend Blair, who gave me my first (and still most) meaningful goal: Strive to create a consequential introduction each day—not a "SMART" one but a meaningful one that moves, drives, and impacts the people I'm introducing. A goal like that not only connects my story and my why, but connects directly to the goal of my business to harness the power of authentic and caring relationships to build connections and generate results.

Meaningful goals can do the same for you and your millennials. But how you communicate, understand, and respect the goals will be essential, because you want to push your millennials to do the same. Yes, push. As I said before, this two-way street of accountability now requires millennials to clean up their side of the street and own their goals. You can't just mentor them. They must mentor themselves—ask themselves BIG questions that create shared purpose, hold themselves accountable by asking: *How do I create more meaning in my job? How can I better support the goals of the company? Are there tasks that don't seem to align with the company's and my goals, and if so, what can I do to create alignment?*

If all this sounds like more work than you usually do on your annual goals, then you're right. No more annual "set it and forget it" meetings to discuss goals that you then you never revisit, revise, or reconsider throughout the year. You can't just say what the goals are once a year and expect people to "get it," and for those goals to stay relevant to them. That's a sure way that the dots are never connected, shared purpose is never achieved, and transparency is never enhanced.

Lead with Transparency and Purpose

With the individual and corporate goals now literally laid out in front of everyone, it is the perfect time to ask "What do you share with your team? What do you not share? Why?" Most companies withhold information more and more as they move down the ladder from the C-suite, because that's the way it was as the folks at the top worked their way into the inner sanctum. But millennials—even those at the entry level—

want and expect transparency. Do you let them see in? What are you hiding—and why?

To truly live, value, and communicate individual and corporate goals every day means making sure everything behind those goals is as transparent as possible. That's how you motivate a team of millennials. If they don't see as much of your business and inner workings as possible, they will think you are hiding something, believe you don't have the goods to help them learn and grow, and aren't nimble enough to adapt when things change. Then they will leave—as will your clients and customers, eventually. Yes, customers. Customers want to know you can roll with things strategically as technology and availability of data make the need for speed and reassessment paramount to success. They expect the same level of transparency in order to trust and share their business with you, to create alignment between their goals and yours. They want to know you can deliver results and service that help them meet their goals, but they expect flexibility, adaptability, and communication regularly around those goals or any issues that come up. Like your millennials, they expect communication to be forthcoming and transparent.

In this regard, millennials are your greatest ally. They *are* flexible. They have dealt with constant change all their lives, especially on the technology side, and are fine with course corrections—as long as they understand why changes are being made. To make sure they understand, you must communicate new goals to your millennials, share and guide them through your and the company's thinking behind the goals, and let them own as much as possible as paths to learning, growth, and pushing themselves to be better. Millennials shouldn't control the goals any more than they get to make the rules, but they do expect to be involved and invested in what they are doing, and that means understanding and even helping to shape *why* they are doing something. Share as much as you can about the goals—explain clearly the purpose and meaning of certain organizational goals, why they exist, and how they tie into strengths and core values.

So do you invite them to their own party and deliver on the invitation? Do you have a culture that shares and explains why certain organizational goals exist? Are these as transparent as possible and clearly communicated?

This was not the case with a company I worked with to solve the problem the new chief marketing officer (CMO) had the courage to mess with, the "third rail" of sales: the commission or percentage of each deal her salespeople got. The previous CMO had given out incentives and bonuses for everything but no one ever really understood what was being incentivized or rewarded and as a result they were *not* growing. Moreover, the new CMO noted that the incentives created competition between the staff. So she removed the commission and restructured it into different shared incentives that were transparent and adaptable to all parts of the business. She also scrapped the quarterly bonuses and—gasp!—the big incentive trip that the company went on when it met its revenue goals.

"The trip was an indicator of success but it wasn't shared, as people with families often could not go," the CMO noted. "But that wasn't the only reason. In fact, I did it based on a survey I did of the staff that asked what motivated them. At the bottom of the survey, I wrote, 'Would you rather take a trip with the company or would you rather have money?' At the end of the day, what I got back was surprising and alarming but so simple: They wanted to be appreciated, but money was a huge issue because raises were small and annual at best. So I put together a plan that defined everyone's jobs from the front desk up and made it and a new incentive plan transparent and shared throughout the company. Everyone shared in it, from the front desk people who made $15 an hour up to the managers. The more they did, the more they could generate. It even tied to attitude, punctuality, and ethics, among other things, so everyone pushed everyone else to perform, and everyone was incentivized to share in the purpose of what we were doing."

Did it work? The CMO admitted that the restructuring cost her a few disgruntled employees, but it effectively spurred the others to daily success. And it created trust through transparent recognition and celebration of that success, as everyone understood how and what they contributed. She even tied it in to daily motivational huddles.

Super cool. Super transparent and measurable, too. She had effectively ensured a complete mindset shift from "me" to "we" to achieve those meaningful individual and team goals and now can demonstrate caring on an operationalized and completely results-oriented level. Because *none of this matters without results*. Once you have created shared, aligned, and meaningful goals that are transparent and adaptable, the next step is to define success metrics for those results—making those meaningful goals mean more than just words. In other words, meaningful goals must do more than generate good will and connections. This is about your business delivering value and results, not an exercise in team bonding and charity.

If it doesn't create measurable results, then what's the point? Make sure you have clear success metrics to evaluate the impact of that achievement, and that you can define what success looks like and how will it be measured.

Measure to Create Results

Millennials don't just want transparency to know what's expected. They want to know what success looks like for their roles, team, and company. They want to know how they will be measured, with no surprises, as long as they do what they say they will do to achieve those meaningful goals (and then do it all over again).

Leaders must drive these metrics and ensure they connect to results by

- measuring before they even "get there": Before hiring, make sure you know whether you are getting a good fit, not just a great interview. Then you can, in effect, start training and measuring before "birth," including how well you are hiring.

- helping employees identify their strengths, and ensuring those strengths align with their individual goals
- naming the concrete actions to accomplish those goals, and creating a timeline for accomplishing them
- providing resources and continuous coaching and feedback, and suggesting how resources can be shared
- establishing an accountability plan with follow-up, and engaging employees' development by following up on milestones often and regularly

Start doing this by writing down the targets for those individual goals. Then set regular, periodic check-ins with targets that establish and reaffirm the links between individual performance and team goals, and between team goals and organizational goals/success. Check-ins can be weekly, monthly, quarterly, and annual. Make sure team projects, deadlines, project management, sales goals, benchmarks, processes, procedures, and systems are discussed openly and freely in the way they contribute to measurement.

Goals can and must be moving targets, so sharing and writing down those goals and then discussing and re-evaluating the metrics are important for them to work. This requires both leaders and their teams to take responsibility for capitalizing on the opportunities and delivering results. Don't be afraid to adjust your goals even if that means changing the way work works.

> Clarify, Communicate, Share—Measure!

Then plow the meaningful achievements of those results into new innovations and collaborations. Make communication and brainstorm sessions part of how you measure and outgrowths of every celebrated moment. Are you having these kinds of conversations with your millennials and making each success a chance to innovate? If not, create group and team activities that enable managers and millennials to collaborate to address situations, scenarios, and business goals, and have teams then share results of their collaboration. Take pride in them!

That's how you create a team of problem solvers and innovators with a shared purpose. That's how you avoid letting the *idea* of caring enough to forge relationships and authentic connections, breaking through barriers, owning problems, delivering value, and understanding the need for meaningful shared goals end up being a bunch of words in a business plan, disconnected from reality. Now you just need to build a plan that maintains those goals and ensures everyone understands and embraces the vision of the company.

It was one of the lowest tech businesses I have ever visited that showed me just how successful a business can be by making and measuring meaningful goals in a sustainable way—and thus ensuring that their people embrace the vision of the company through achieving those goals.

LAZ Parking (*http://bit.ly/20OgT2z*) started in 1981 when its CEO Alan Lazowski launched a small business parking cars at a restaurant in his hometown of Hartford, Connecticut, while he was in college. Today, it is one of the world's largest parking companies, with valet services at thousands of garages, clubs, hotels, and other locations nationwide and worldwide with Indigo (formerly Vinci Park). The residents and guests at those locations may be high-tech millionaires, but LAZ isn't a high technology company. It is a parking company with lots and garages that look nothing like the auto "silo" in which Tom Cruise saved the world in *Mission Impossible—Ghost Protocol*. There is nothing revolutionary about their service. Whether it is serving one of the original Hartford locations or one of the hottest hotels in Hollywood, LAZ is a model for all of us: They know the success of their services and thus their company comes down to one thing . . . *people.*

And thousands of those people who work for LAZ are millennials— some temporarily, some as a path to experience as managers, to build careers within and beyond the company, and all of them with expectations and issues that would feel familiar to anyone who employs them. Yet LAZ has continued to expand and thrive in a high-pressure, high-turnover business with mostly positive references from the people who work for them and the clients they serve. Why? Because LAZ models caring about people as central to its corporate values. They call it "The People Model": inspirational leadership; results-driven leadership; authentic and effective communication; and collaborative innovation. They make it clear that the rules of the model "are the rules we expect the LAZ family to play by, the rules that form the character of our company."

Note those words: "we" and "family" and "our." This is a company with a model and mission, values and practices, that B.R.I.D.G.E.s the gap in all but its name: They have behaviors, measurements, and actions that promote those values, including a get-connected program they recently started. I sat through one of these programs, in which leaders from around the country share stories with the entire C-suite. These stories were not about what The People Model means to them; they were *about people*. That day there were fifty people in the room, many of them millennials—forty-five of whom were new to the company within the past three years, making these connecting programs essential for real-deal relationships. Yes, they also talked about how they feel supported, and how the company can better support them. But it started and ended with the most personal of stories. And they were very real—everyone shared and then connected them to why they do what they do, including the founder of LAZ who told his parents' story about surviving the Holocaust.

In effect, I saw at LAZ a major part of our inside-out program at launchbox—communicating your story—working in a real millennial management program at one of the largest companies of its kind in the world. And the goals were the same as ours. From the top down, LAZ wants to know as much as it can about everything, and its culture reflects this caring—right down to the hugging. In the hallways before and after the program, I found it astonishing how much everyone was genuinely hugging everyone—and I'm a hugger! It didn't matter if you just met or were seeing an old friend—you meet 'em, you hug 'em. And if you don't know them, you start right then by asking what they do, who they work for, and what property they work at. Okay, hugging for you can be optional. But not the rest.

Is LAZ a perfect company? No. Does LAZ know that some of its employees—be they entry-level or managers—will chafe under these demands and stress of the job? Of course. That mistakes will happen? Yes. But given how many operations LAZ runs in a business that can be as thankless as any, I was impressed at just how meaningful and genuine these goals were to its employees and how few complaints they seem to have. To me, this is all a perfect example of how you celebrate, innovate, and drive accountability to goals—especially in a business that is by and large transactional and thus limited in its ability to reinvent the way business is done.

I don't want you to imitate LAZ—or any company in this book—but understand how it works for you and create something similar for you and your company/millennials. *Write out a plan to build and maintain your meaningful goals and then live them and own them.*

You don't need to call what you're doing B.R.I.D.G.E. or The People Program to have everything we have talked about come together through this point. In the end, it has to be your program, not mine. You just have to back up the meaningful words behind the meaningful goals with meaningful actions that are meaningful to your people. And only by embracing and committing to those goals with this level of transparency, alignment, measurement, collaboration, and innovation will your millennials care about how much you know because they know how much you care.

That's how you embrace their vision and in turn have them embrace yours.

MAKE IT HAPPEN:
Create Alignment Between Shared Individual and Team Goals

I have had some BHAG (big hairy audacious goals) personally and professionally—for both myself and others—in my life. But it wasn't until I really understood the power of aligning and sharing individual, team, and company goals and making them meaningful that I truly understood how to achieve them by moving from "me" to "we." You must make others' goals a central part of your world, particularly through how you engage and align individual goals with the team's and company's goals to show that you care.

What can you do tomorrow to create alignment around shared goals for your millennials?

1. **Have a shared vision and shared goals** that create alignment between individuals, team, and company. Connect the dots. Show that you care about where they and the company are going, not just what they are doing, by connecting what you need them to do to their "why."

2. **Lead with transparency and purpose** to increase engagement and trust. Embracing *meaningful* goals not only shows millennials how much you care, but further ensures that you embrace their vision and in turn have them embrace yours.

3. **Measure to create results.** Don't just establish the link between individual performance and team goals as well as organizational goals/success; have metrics for progress toward them and then plow achievements into new collaborations and innovations. Build a plan to maintain them and to ensure individuals and teams that embrace the vision for the company. Write them out and own them top to bottom!

E: Empower Success

Empower your culture and employees to drive results.

#feedback365 #reward

Looking over a list of people I needed to thank at the end of launchbox's first year, I kept being drawn to one name: Mary Johnson. I had met Mary when I started my job in the auto business. I took her culture course with my HR director, and I could just tell she was awesome. Older and more experienced than me, Mary was eventually hired as a consultant to help build the culture we needed at the company, and the work she did with us—from defining strengths and core values to creating an open and transparent environment—continues to define who I am as a leader and what I want to do for others today.

Because she meant so much to me, I really spent time crafting Mary's thank-you. I told her she was the first person who introduced me to what became my work at launchbox. I said I never knew how to operationalize what I was doing until our work together, and that she had pushed me to discover in new ways how much I loved growing and teaching people, helping them get out of their own way to get results. Finally, I wrote about how she as much as anyone drove me to create launchbox—my team and I had created a growing business in part around what I had learned from her.

"We've got something here, something really special," I wrote. "Thank you for doing what you did for me and setting me on my true path."

I never got a response.

Two months later, a speech I gave caught the attention of the chief culture officer at LAZ Parking, who I heard was considering me for a gig. And who do I find out was consulting for that LAZ executive? Mary. When she heard about me from the chief culture officer, she called and apologized for not responding to the email, and invited me to lunch.

The lunch started the way lunches do when two people who have been close reunite after a time. We talked about kids and grandkids, former colleagues, what we'd been doing since we last met. That's not because Mary was avoiding the tough conversations but because that's the way Mary taught me to interact and the way she still interacts today. She calls it "Human : Business : Human." Start with what bonds us (with what is human), then conduct business, and then end with a human interaction. In our social media-saturated world where talking at each other passes for being human, Mary's "Human : Business : Human" has never felt more important to me.

I told Mary more about launchbox, what we did together, and how my team and I had evolved from the days of coaching my son and his friends into a real business founded on the principles she taught me, and I thanked her again for all she did for me. Mary smiled and I thought, "Okay, here comes the business."

"Not only was that thank-you amazing, but when I got the call about your coming to speak at the company I thought, 'Dan Negroni is a great guy. How could I not love Dan Negroni.'"

Super nice.

"But you know, I just have to be honest with you because we have that type of relationship . . . then I thought, 'I don't know about Dan Negroni. He'd be great for us unless he brings all that ego with him.'"

Um . . . *what? Ouch!* That hurt.

"And," she continued, "I just have to tell you that sitting here with you today has been one of the coolest experiences. How happy am I to be able to go tell them that there is a different Dan Negroni sitting in front of me? The humility you show and how passionate you are about what you are doing and how you want to help people is so heartwarming and exactly what you needed to be as amazing as you are now."

Wow.

She was right, too. About everything.

When I worked with Mary, I was making millions. I "had it all": the jet, the car, the house . . . and the ego to boot. I was doing a lot of things right. I cared enough about the culture of the business to work with Mary and develop the core values that supported my people, their strengths, and sustainable growth. On paper, it all worked. Every team meeting was energetic, every event fun, every sales quarter a record. But it was about "me" not "we" first. What did my ego care about being other-directed? I didn't think about others or being humble when I walked out to my personalized parking spot where my car was detailed whenever I wanted. I was not mature enough to have or even know the importance of humility in empowering others to succeed. I was thirty-five and I was arrogant.

That was the "me" Mary remembered. She had seen the good things, too—a leader who believed in doing the right things by his people and the company he worked for— and often did—but at the center of it all was me: a guy on a power trip, the one who had not moved from "me" to "we." I may have been a good manager but I could have been so much better at empowering success if I had just kept my ego in check.

In fact, it wasn't until the first time I spent the day with my dad at launchbox, watching him walk around and engage with the team and the space, that I realized how much better I was today—how amazing it feels to create and be a part of a business where I can be 100 percent me and own it. In every job I have ever had before I started this one, I have played "the game" and suppressed at least a part of who I was for what I thought, or "they" thought, I was supposed to be and do. I found it limiting, and as a result my ego flared. I never saw the wisdom in being any other way. Today, I am responsible and accountable to myself for empowering everyone I connect to and with everything I touch. It is nothing short of amazing that my team and I get to do what we want to do and say what we feel all day, every day, while creating super value and empowerment for each other, our families, friends, clients, and especially our ~~millennials~~ next-generation leaders.

I get to be the jolter and stimulator, the coach, the mentor, and learner all in one. It does not get better than that.

Does that mean my ego is gone today? Hardly. I'm still (a little) vain and drive an expensive car and love my watch du jour. But I instinctively appreciate that relationships are the most important thing in life. I value meaningful connections, making it about others, and the power to create and work with millennials to both lead and be led by me and my team, because we are mastering learning to work from the inside out. I was careless before. Today I choose to care more. Today Mary and all of the clients and customers we serve care

> Empower the culture and employees to drive results.

about what we know because they know first and foremost how much we care. And I'm intense about it, especially when it comes to empowerment. I empower people to succeed 24/7 and expect empowerment from them in return—we study it, live it, teach it, technologize it, and *love it.*

Are you empowering and engaging your employees to be successful? Are they engaged and empowered so you can do your job successfully? When you can answer these questions with a resounding "Yes!" you have empowered success by empowering your employees to develop a culture that you can be proud of. Now reinforce that empowerment and

✓ **Focus on individual growth.** Care more by assessing
and leveraging individual strengths as a path to
delivering value and results for your team, company,
and clients

✓ **Pave the road.** Give them what they need to be successful.

✓ **Give "Feedback 365."** Now . . . always!

✓ **Recognize and celebrate** more than just the goals
achieved.

These are the things you must start doing tomorrow to empower
your culture and your millennials to succeed.

Focus on Individual Growth

The problem at a large client of ours centered on money, namely the jeal-
ousies it had created in the office. As is usually the case when it comes
to situations like this, there was a ton of backstabbing going on—people
criticizing each other while feigning friendship (one of the ultimate
forms of inauthenticity). The lack of trust that resulted was toxic. Yet
this was a national Top 25 company in its field—prestigious and high
volume, with revenue to match. But while the numbers at the company
seemed strong, it was like crops growing in contaminated water: It
doesn't matter how healthy the spinach you produce is, because people
will (eventually) get sick eating something good for them.

Not surprisingly, it was the chief financial officer (CFO) who discovered the truth beneath the numbers, and the source of the problem: the
chief operations officer (COO). The COO had created an organizational
chart that, instead of being distributed evenly with several managers
leading teams, had everyone reporting to one person: the COO. And the
COO reported only to the CEO, who trusted the COO for everything.

Now, the COO had been there a long time, and he was by all counts
a good person, but his managing style was "sweep it under the rug."

Instead of being straight with everyone, he pandered to everyone's whims and speciously played everyone against the middle, pitting everyone's interests against one another. This created havoc, unfair treatment, favorites, and challenges that went right back to the top, which the COO ducked and covered up with more deception. He told people what they wanted to hear about the problems they had and never addressed the injury or causes with more than a Band-Aid, if at all. This entire mess he had managed to hide from the CEO, which left the CFO who saw it all happening powerless to help.

Drama eventually started to build as the problems became more and more apparent. And when the COO knew things were going down? That COO quit. He just left. Walked out on Friday and never came back, sending his resignation via email.

Good. *He had to go.*

We ended up consulting for the company when the CFO stepped into the COO role and needed help rebuilding trust. He had taken it upon himself to restructure everything and encouraged direct and authentic conversations while he did. That's when everything that had been swept under the rug started to fly around the office and all the Band-Aids started to pop off. The bleeding could not be controlled.

> Does everyone understand expectations and have the power/authority to do their jobs?

"It was everywhere in the company," the CFO told me. "All at once. I had two to three months of people complaining about promises made to them that were not delivered. Some were reasonable, but some of those promises? They were ridiculous and I became a hard ass. I said, "No! That is not the way it is going to work here." I managed with an iron fist but with a lot of love, too. I was strict but compassionate—the same way I am with my kids. I was understanding but direct. I was diligent about communicating what needed to be done. The problem was they had trusted someone with false promises that gave the illusion of empowerment but nothing had been delivered, and now they lacked trust in anything that was told to them."

It took the CFO three months to stop that bleeding. And he did it by making sure his largely millennial staff was, in the words of Jim Collins in *Good to Great*, "in the right seats on the bus" by creating a system to assess and leverage strengths by

- aligning tasks with employee competencies
- creating systems to identify high-potential employees and challenge them
- focusing on and helping employees develop their strengths
- creating growth opportunities for high-flight risks

First, he made sure the right people were in the right jobs and were set up for success. He hired practice managers to oversee the two working managers in the office, because these managers were also technicians and did not have time to manage.

"I told them they were no longer managers and they took it badly," the CFO said. "They felt like they were being demoted but I told them they had been set up to fail, doing mediocre jobs with opposing responsibilities. I wanted to make them the great medical assistants they were and set them up to succeed. I knew it would be a good change, starting with reducing their eleven-hour workdays. I also knew it would take time and attention, which is why I let the practice managers lead from their strengths and manage them, not me."

In the end, the CFO did this with everyone. He refused to let the team run over him like the old COO, who had spoiled the people by never holding them or himself accountable to a culture that actually empowered them to do their jobs. That's why some of them grated against the new program that required accountability and leadership; no one had ever held them to any standard before. As a result, they always wanted more whether they deserved it or not. The CFO made them take a hard look at themselves and challenged them. And while some people had to be let go, the highest potential employees thrived.

To make sure those people were happy, he went around the office every day and showed his concern, asking about their day, noticing when they were unhappy and working to address it with a checklist of responsibilities and guidelines. They were now trained on what they were supposed to do, and doing what they were passionate about. As a result, his people were getting their work done in a timely manner without resistance or a bad attitude, and they saw clear opportunities to grow.

> Leverage the best in everyone—assess each individual's strengths, skills, and passions, matching them to tasks, projects, and roles.

Triage is still happening at this company but on the backs of a happier workforce. And they still had their best year ever financially—a year that started with a team of disenfranchised workers and ended with everyone from the CEO down willing to take a new approach that focuses on empowerment—even giving up some of their incentives from the past for a different approach. The CFO did all of this by leading through and leveraging strengths and forcing everyone to be accountable for the resulting success.

To his credit, the CFO never said all this would be easy. In fact, it was the opposite: He pushed them to accept and/or ask for challenging opportunities, making sure they had his ear and the tools they needed to be successful. He had started to pave the road to sustainable success.

Pave the Road

Do you and your employees have what you and they need to be successful? This is a much more loaded question than it seems. We need to figure out how to maximize our millennials' contributions to grow our businesses, because this responsibility extends way beyond our individual business' bottom lines. As I touched on in the introduction, it extends to our homes; that's where many of us are likely to see millennials long after they graduate from college as they struggle with crippling student debt and stagnant wages.

According to the *New York Times*, during the most recent recession, "[millennials] moved in with their parents in record numbers. Now jobs may be more plentiful and the economy has improved, but many members of the millennial generation have yet to leave the nest." In fact, even more of them are living at home now: An analysis of census data by the Pew Research Center found that eighteen- to thirty-four-year-olds are less likely to be living apart from family members than they were even during the depths of the recent recession, the worst economic downturn since the 1930s.

"Young adults were the age group that was hardest hit by the Great Recession," says Richard Fry, a senior researcher at the Pew Research Center. "They're not fully healed from the damages." Or as Steven Rattner, a Wall Street executive, noted in the *New York Times*, "[We should] be fretful over their economic well-being and fearful—oh so fearful—for their prospects. The most educated generation in history is on track to becoming less prosperous, at least financially, than its predecessors."

That said, in 2015 an NPR story challenged the idea that millennials suffer from higher rates of depression and similar mental health issues because of this. They do have challenges with conflict negotiation and find it difficult to think for themselves, in part because of what we discussed in Part One: Mom and Dad made things very easy by being in the cure business rather than the story business. But millennials are not depressed or ashamed about the hands they have been dealt. They are perfectly willing to live in their parents' basements or move from sofa to sofa while they "gig" and look for good jobs, refusing to pile up the credit card debt of generations before.

Still, that same story on NPR noted millennials are anxious and lack trust in non-millennials to find the solutions. Can you blame them? This is why we must keep paving the road. We've been careless with millennials and our overall future for too long. We must pave the road not only to empower them to succeed but also to reaffirm the trust we have established through the work so far.

Ask yourself: Are you the leader your millennials need you to be to empower success and build trust?

- Define expectations and then delegate authority, providing the tools, resources, information, and direction they need to do the job and do it dynamically, adjusting as expectations, goals, and situations change.
- Be prepared, resolve conflicts, and encourage participation and sharing of opinion.
- Then get out of the cure business and let them work; step back and have their backs when it comes to the rest of the organization.

Pave the road to success but don't cure your millennials' problems— make them take responsibility for their own empowerment.

Because as I have said before, this paved road is a two-way street now and your team must be able to keep their paved side clean to empower themselves and build trust with their leaders.

Millennials must ask: *Am I the employee my manager needs me to be?* Millennials can't be afraid to ask for help and the tools, resources, information, and direction they need to do their jobs. They must take responsibility for understanding what is expected, be prepared to clarify and manage expectations, and communicate important decisions, issues, and progress as they go. You want them to seize and seek out opportunities to support the work of you and the team, and then do what they say they will do when they say they will do it. Don't just delegate; make them want your job! Growth opportunities equal retention; make sure future advancement opportunities are transparently available.

As you learned to do in the "B: Bust Myths" chapter, to accept all this and act in the right way, millennials must now assume positive intent (API) and deliver consistently and constantly with no surprises; become active participants in team meetings and discussions; and back up the team and you. And the most direct path to reinforce it is through feedback.

Feedback 365

How many times have you sent an email or posted a question online about a product or service and gotten annoyed when it took more than an hour to get a response? Or how about having to wait to talk to customer service because "call volume is higher than normal." Or being number 57 as the deli clerk calls "32." Or clicking "refresh" over and over on your kid's summer camp Facebook page, annoyed because they haven't posted the latest round of pictures that might include your child?

You hate it, right? So why don't you understand your millennials' needs for constant feedback? They have never known a world absent of instant gratification and constant communication. The fact that millennials ask for feedback beyond quarterly or annual reviews is not only completely understandable but also a gift you get every day to shape and guide them. They are actually doing you a favor. How about that for an API mindset?

Does your company have a mandate to connect and give direct feedback regularly (daily, weekly, after each important project)? Do you ask for feedback in return, to model how to receive that feedback? Do you have an open-door policy? Are you in huddles each morning? Are you doing "drive-bys" all day long, trying to catch them doing something right? Are you always just a text away from any challenge to guide, lead, or lean in? Do you practice real-deal conversations with great questions? If not, then you don't have "Feedback 365": the unwavering belief and desire to deliver and receive feedback every day, all year long, as an essential part of your internal communication. Do this and do it right—consistently, honestly, and "carefrontationally"—and you let your people know not only where they stand but also where you stand with them, which leads to empowerment for all. Leaders need to fuel this and individualize it across the company, top to bottom. Someone in shipping may not aspire to the same things as a senior manager, but they both aspire to be noticed, feel like part of a team, and know that someone cares about them.

Millennials have the most to learn about taking responsibility in this regard, especially when it comes to asking for what they want using the power of questions—namely asking for it instead of assuming they won't get it or that no one wants to give it. I did a seminar for a multibillion-dollar-company, and one employee said, "I don't understand how I am doing and no one is telling me how I'm doing." I said, "Okay, what do

> Provide and ask for regular feedback on performance all day, every day.

you do about that?" And I got a blank look from her. "Let me give you a tip," I continued. "If you want feedback, then go ahead and stop whining and ask for it." Any employee who complains about not getting feedback without having asked for it is going to get an earful from me—as is the manager of that person if there is no mandate to give it.

When and how will you give the constructive feedback you'd like to provide to someone at work? When and how will you ask for what you need to do your job better?

These questions always go together, because "Feedback 365" is always a balance between give and take.

THE GIVE AND TAKE OF FEEDBACK

GIVE

- Ask permission
- Be a giver leader—have their back
- Ask great questions, seek to understand
- Appreciate their efforts
- Align with goals and results
- Give support / stories / examples
- Lose the "back in my day"
- Check in / drive by / huddle on progress and improvements

TAKE
- Practice active listening skills
- Lose defensiveness and judgment
- Ask for specific examples
- Paraphrase back and be empathetic
- Thank them for feedback
- Focus on "cleaning your side of the street"

If the feedback involves a tough conversation, don't hide from it. Choose those tough conversations wisely, though, and remember the power of asking great questions that we covered in "I: I Own It." Sometimes it is better to hold back and ask questions first to determine if the conversation is worth it, using all the skills you have developed so far in B.R.I.D.G.E. Ask yourself

- Is it really about them?
- Is it better for them to change or me?
- Is my purpose clear?
- Is the feedback only short-term release?
- Is it accepting of others?
- Is my intent clear?

In the words of the Kenny Rogers song "The Gambler" (millennials will know him from the GEICO ad), you gotta know when to fold 'em—and you must fold on the tough conversation if the answer to any of these questions is "no." When the answers are all "yes," go ahead and hold 'em. Hold the tough conversations but adhere to the following rules.

- Let go of the past.
- Stick to facts.
- Use the power of the question.
- Be constructive.
- Be firm.
- Explore solutions.

The good news is that like so many aspects of B.R.I.D.G.E., feed-back is something that can be practiced. In fact, you can even role-play asking for what you need and giving constructive feedback with other leaders and even millennials to prepare for the conversation. Try different approaches and responses, and ask, "What worked? What didn't?" You can even make learning how to live and give "Feedback 365" through an exercise we do for many of our clients called "You Moved Me."

EXERCISE:

You Moved Me

1. Each person writes down
   - one thing that you need to ask for to do your job better (e.g. "I need more of your time to share my ideas.")
   - constructive feedback that you would like to provide to someone at work (e.g. "What you said was interesting but you need to slow down and breathe.")
2. Standing in mixed pairs (try and mix up age, gender/ gender identification, race, job level, etc. wherever possible), hands to hands—pushing!—start practicing.
   - Person #1: Bring up a live action (one thing you wrote down that you need to address that involves someone else) and discuss it.
   - Person #2: Listen to Person #1's attempt to discuss their action.
   - If Person #2 likes the way Person #1 addressed the action, Person #2 releases the tension between their hands: Person #2 has been "moved."
   - If Person #2 does *not* like the way Person #1 addressed the action, tension stays the same and Person #1 tries again until they move Person #2.

3. When you have been moved, discuss *why*; focus on behaviors and the words actually said. (Rarely, someone will not or cannot be moved. If someone is not moved after a few tries, stop and ask for feedback. If that person is still not moved, you are at an impasse. But still discuss what happened and why.)

4. Now switch. Start from the beginning with Person #2 bringing up an action.

5. After everyone has practiced what is on their list, in groups of two pairs discuss each person's shared learning.
   - What I could have done better was . . .
   - What I liked about what someone else did was . . .

6. After short discussions, bring the whole group together and do SHOUT OUTS!
   - What did you like that someone else did? What worked well and why?
   - What could you have done better? What could they have done better?

Doing an exercise like "You Moved Me" only works when you make time to commit to it, which is the case with "Feedback 365." After all, pick a day. I bet it is one of the 365! Actually, there is a line between giving and taking feedback all the time and overusing it. I don't want you literally to give it every day. That's just as inauthentic as saying "I'm sorry" for something before you know what you did, and just as annoying as a fly buzzing around your head.

Don't make your millennials feel like the one who wrote me

It's damn near impossible to ask for more feedback on whether or not a single thing I did for them was helpful or to please be more involved or at least kept in the loop when things happen, because I know that they simply don't have the time or value doing that. I'm not dumb. I'm aware of their hectic days, and I know that the feedback (like teaching and mentoring) is at the very bottom of the priority list. I completely understand why that's the case. I just don't know why they don't.

Make feedback part of your culture and tie it into your style of management so there are no surprises, no suspicions. I want you to remember your active listening techniques from the "R: Real Deal" chapter: When you give someone feedback, you listen because you know how you feel when someone else doesn't. Listening during feedback makes someone feel important—and compels the other person to listen back as genuinely as you did.

And when they do? I hope they hear something good.

Recognize and Celebrate

Remember the CMO client I mentioned in the "G: Goals in Mind" chapter who got rid of the company's existing commissions, goals, and incentives and instead focused on what mattered to her people *today*? That's also an essential step in empowering success. At the end of the day, we are so focused on what's next, we sometimes forget about making space for celebrating today as a source of empowerment. Even when we celebrate and recognize achieving big and small goals, we can't forget what's happening now. In fact, according to a joint survey by Achievers and Experience, Inc., "Eighty percent of [millennials] said they prefer on-the-spot recognition over formal reviews, and feel that this is imperative for their growth and understanding of a job."

Do you celebrate short-term wins, individual contributions, and team successes, and do it publicly in a fun, creative, and interactive team culture?

Do you do this? Ask yourself and your company

- Are you rewarding the behaviors you want?
- Are you getting those behaviors?
- Is there anyone at work that you should recognize for his/her contributions?

If the answer to any of these questions is "no," then you are neither rewarding the behaviors you want nor giving your millennials what they need. You don't have their backs. So try the following exercise. It should sound familiar if you remember the promise I made to you at the start of this book. Now it is time to pay it forward.

EXERCISE:
I Have Your Back

1. In a large group, have everyone tape a piece of paper on their backs.
2. Have everyone grab a marker, move around the room, and write either a strength they see in that person or a word or phrase that describes what they appreciate about that person on their back.
3. See how much they have your back: Take off the pieces of paper and read them aloud.
4. Smile and wonder why you needed to tape a piece of paper to everyone's back to recognize and celebrate achievements in the way individuals want to be recognized.

So go ahead—*make their day with some recognition!* You have no idea what day people have had. Change your approach and be the one who shifts their day! What's more empowering and fun than that?

Yes, I said *fun*. This can and should be fun. I hope it has been fun for you. And inspiring. And maddening. And not a little bit confusing, too. Because it can be confusing. Consider this note a millennial client of mine wrote to her manager as part of her work at launchbox

> Don't tell me what to do step by step or send me detailed instructions. Come on just frame the issue for me. Give me guidance and tell me to run with it. Trust me. Then don't just hide and blow me off. Do check-ins. Make sure I am okay. Wouldn't you want that? Sometimes you just kick me to the curb and forget about me and I am stuck. So uncool.

How confusing is that? Don't tell me what to do but give me guidance. Be there for me along the way—but not too much. I don't want you hovering or smothering me—but don't forget because I'm going to get upset.

This is all confusing. And I love it. Every little last bit of it. Millennials have forced us to reconsider how we do things and what we need to be for them and we love them—and hate them—for it, too. It *is* confusing. As confusing as Justin Bieber.

Yes, I said Justin Bieber.

> Train, Teach, Learn:
> They want guides.
> We want to guide.

To me, Justin Bieber epitomizes the challenges we face with millennials in our world today. Is he a good guy or bad guy? You tell me. Is he an idiot? A thug? Or is he a philanthropist? Is he a symbol and mouthpiece for youthful disorder with 61 million Twitter followers? An uncontrollable musical talent? A protégé of Usher? A womanizer? A sensitive young man who wears his heart on his sleeve? An entrepreneur? The best brand ambassador Calvin Klein ever had?

Yes, yes, yes, yes, yes . . . Justin Bieber is all these things. He is everything that is good—and bad—about millennials. And the only way to reconcile the confusion is to be the coach, mentor, and learner all at once, accept that this confluence of youth and experience cannot be controlled by the way things were, and let it flourish.

We can't ever reconcile it. We just enable it by creating a culture of disruption and learning—an environment where communication and education also mean calling everyone (yes, yourself included) on their shit. Which means the final step of empowerment brings us back to where we started: Get out of your own way.

You've spent too long focused on you. Go back to the beginning and be that Giver Leader—that other-directed person—and bridge this gap.

MAKE IT HAPPEN:
I Empower My Team to Succeed

It took a long time for me to truly understand how to put the pieces together to empower individuals and myself to be better and in turn make one another better by paving the road and never sacrificing what was right for what was easy. When it worked? It was beautiful. When it didn't? It was still pretty great just trying to do things the right way.

What can you do tomorrow to empower your culture and employees to succeed? To develop a culture that you can be proud of and that empowers you to do your job successfully?

1. **Focus on individual growth.** Manage each person differently, align tasks with employee competencies, focus on and help employees develop their strengths, and create a system to identify high-potential employees, challenge them, and create growth opportunities.
2. **Pave the road** by ensuring your millennials have what they need to be successful. Make sure delegation and creating trust are givens, and make them want your job. Make future advancement opportunities transparently available.
3. **"Feedback 365":** Do it daily and never stop; provide and ask for regular feedback on performance. Be specific and listen.
4. **Recognize and celebrate** in a fun, creative, and interactive team culture that empowers more success and recognition. Do it for short-term wins, individual contributions, and team successes, in a public way.

Launch Plan

Remember when I first introduced you to B.R.I.D.G.E. and said it would launch you to success by providing a recipe and cooking lesson combined? Well, now you have all the inside-out ingredients from Part One and the lessons from Part Two to create not merely a dish but a feast to serve others. Not just millennials—and not just for a day but sustainably for months and years. As a result, you have also learned the steps and created tools to find your own relevance and connect with and create next-generation leaders.

So . . . what are you going to do right now to create and empower the next generation of leaders? How can you become one yourself and be the guide? Those are the questions I asked myself before I wrote this book, and they are the questions I ask you as I end it. Don't just read them—*answer them and act.* What are you going to do to get you and your people across the B.R.I.D.G.E.?

Here is your commitment plan. *Start, do, be, repeat!*

Bust myths to identify and break through underlying assumptions about employees that create barriers by

- not making assumptions when dealing with other generations—we are more the same than different.
- understanding and valuing different work needs, values, and styles
- focusing on and assuming positive intent

Create **real-deal** authentic, caring relationships with your team by

- connecting authentically and creating real emotional connections, showing genuine interest and caring for others
- sharing your friggin' self
- practicing questioning, asking great questions, and really being willing to have tough conversations
- showing gratitude by incorporating humility and thankfulness into your habits

Demonstrate an **I own it** mindset that forces you to be personally accountable and responsible for driving results by

- understanding your strengths and your story; once you get yourself you can impact others and lead teams
- choosing your mindset by taking personal ownership for what and how things happen to you
- taking personal accountability and measuring yourself on how well you do this, daily

Deliver value through understanding, mentorship, and coaching of others by

- being the right kind of giver; choosing Giver Leadership in everything you say and do; being focused on the how
- shifting to mentor and remembering that you are the Giver Leader and a role model

- making it about others, remembering that you are not the hero of your own story, and getting rid of the part of your ego that holds you back

Keep **goals in mind** based on a shared and embraced vision by
- creating a shared vision, shared purpose, and shared goals that align those of individuals, the team, and the company
- creating meaningful goals and priorities
- building and maintaining goals for the individual and team that compel everyone to embrace the vision of the company

Empower success by
- focusing on individual growth and caring more about assessing the team's strengths
- paving the road and giving individuals what they need to be successful
- giving "Feedback 365"
- recognizing and celebrating often, contextually, and individually as well as with a team focus

CONCLUSION

It's Your Turn

My client, the head of business development at an engineering firm, was pleased but confused. "Why is launchbox so good at this and I am not?" she asked. "Every millennial or manager we have sent to you to coach and train intensively, you have turned around. Made them better salespeople, managers, and employees. I'm not saying I'm unhappy. I'm just wondering "Why can't we do this ourselves? Why can your team have such an impact on them? Why do they struggle here but then shift, take accountability, and grow with you there and then come back and succeed with us in the workplace?"

I accepted my client's compliment on behalf of our team and coaches at launchbox. I told her that on the one hand, she should not take it personally; in some ways, it is always easier for consultants to enable the work we do because we lack our clients' internal baggage. On the other hand, the bigger answer was personal. They *could* do it themselves if they worked the same way we do: from the inside out, from self to others to results. That's what gets millennials, managers, and executives right up to the C-level to trust us—not the fact that we are not their employer. In fact, they know we are an agent of their employer. Yet they also know from the moment we step to the table that we see them as individuals. Our goal is first and foremost about them learning to trust and learn from themselves. Because when we call them on their shit and pepper in the corporate stuff to connect what they do to the work of the company, we need our work to be built on the foundation of that trust.

Our client, and all of the clients we work with, to some degree do exactly the opposite. They figure out what the brand is, what the company wants, and what the job descriptions are to support that, and then they apply all that to the individual. That is *not* how you create shared ownership. That is not going to allow your millennials to own their individual strengths, skills, goals, personal brands, and stories and apply them to your business in the workplace and marketplace. That is not telling millennials like it is and calling them on their stuff. That is not the foundation for trust.

That is not how you find internal relevance and how your millennials, managers, and C-level executives find it in you.

"Okay," my client said when I told her this. "How do you guys teach us how to do that when you are not there?"

Well, that's what this book just did.

Now it's your turn.

It has been a long road to get to this place where (most of the time) I am focused on helping others, opening up to their possibilities, and contributing to their success. I am the perpetual "got your back" guy, and launchbox is the perpetual got your back organization, but the truth is? I still fail and am still learning to accept that I will fail, drift, and stray from my commitment to the principles in this book. This is why I not only need to mentor myself but also surround myself with tough mentors and a community that keeps me honest and moving forward.

That movement has led me to great opportunities and experiences, especially through volunteering. I volunteer the way I parent, coach, and work: boldly, generously, and with a focus on empowerment. And one of the organizations I have had the privilege to be involved with is the Challenged Athletes Foundation (CAF).

CAF assists, supports, and provides opportunities for people with physical disabilities to be athletes so they can lead active lifestyles and compete in events. The amazing feeling I get when I am working with CAF is the same one I strive to bring to the table for all of my clients, friends, and colleagues. It reminds me of when I was a little boy overcoming all the "nos" and my abusive situation, and it fuels my drive to be a giving person and leader. CAF events are about conquering fear and becoming everything you want to be. They force you to be in the service of others, which is why my work with CAF is a huge part of my journey to find my purpose. The events are also exercises in humility. To see what these amazing humans do missing one or both arms or legs compared to what I can do with all four of mine? That's humbling.

But even more impressive is who they are and what they mean to me—they compel me to remember all I have yet to accomplish. Never was this clearer than when I took part in the CAF Back to Back New York Cycling Challenge in October 2015: a hundred-mile-plus bike ride from the Intrepid Sea, Air & Space Museum on the west side of New York City to West Point and back with CAF athletes, volunteers, and wounded warriors from all generations and conflicts since Vietnam. I had participated in these types of CAF events, like the Million Dollar Challenge in California, three times before, and that year it coincided with my fiftieth birthday, when I was supposed to spend the day with family and friends. So I decided to meet up with and offer my support to the CAF people but instead do a shorter ride in my hometown of New York City, a ride through where I grew up while fighting to become the man I knew I had to be.

As soon as I arrived at the hotel and saw my CAF family, that plan became moot.

I started to feel something that eventually became the title of this book. I felt that by doing the New York City ride, I would understand more about the relevance I had been chasing for so long—the man I wanted to become and the things I had to offer to help shape people to be their best selves and connect them to one another. I decided to do it after all.

The volunteers that rainy, blustery day included business leaders like me as well as representatives from the sponsors, professors, community leaders, and twenty-five West Point cadets from the triathlon team: Jenny, whose dad owns a candy store in Wisconsin; Todd from New

Jersey, who was all about military service from the day he was born; Emmitt from Ohio, who wanted to be an entrepreneur . . . Together on that ride we were the very intersection of youth and experience—and seeing everyone working together so fluidly was exhilarating. I couldn't help thinking it was exactly what we need to do in the workplace to build next-generation leaders. I couldn't wait to make what I was seeing and learning part of my presentations.

Turns out, I still had so much to learn and experience that weekend.

As we overcame the water and wind and reached West Point, I got to spend even more time with the cadets during our tour of the campus and our meal in the Hogwarts-style dining hall. They all amazed me as genuine next-generation leaders who cared about connecting. They struck me as the giving leaders of the future and they all gave me hope, but none more than the leader of the West Point triathlon club. His name was Alex, and while we were in line at the buffet, he told me he was just getting back into the swing of things because he was recovering from cancer. I asked him what kind and (small cancer world!) we discovered we had both conquered the exact same kind. We swapped stories and showed our scars that ran from our chests to our navels. What we shared bound us beyond traditional youth and experience: my twenty-five-year-old scar tissue next to his red and still healing one.

In the morning, Alex and I found each other and decided to ride back to New York City together. As we rode, he told me he had a CAT scan coming up and he asked me, "What can I expect?"

And my answer to Alex was the same I would I give you about what you can expect from this book—what you and the millennials you serve

> When are you going to stop chasing relevance and *find it within?*

can expect as you find relevance and make your way forward together in this world: "You can expect greatness and innovation, fear and doubt, health and wellness. You can expect life to happen to you, but this experience will make you stronger."

I also told Alex what I told you at the very beginning of the book: If he needed anyone to talk to, I was there for him. "I've got your back. I'll be your man. I will be your guide."

That's what I have tried to be for you on the pages of this book, and now it's time for you to face your own greatness, fear, and doubt, and find your personal relevance to create and connect with next-generation leaders. Understand them. Push them. Guide and be guided. And become one yourself.

Yeah, it's confusing, but what are *you* going to do about it? This is a tougher, faster, more globally competitive world with bigger stakes than any generation before has faced. Millennials demand transparency and purpose.

It's your turn to do what we all have a responsibility to do: Make a difference by finding your Alex and Amanda, John, Corey, Malik, Omar, Youssef, Fatima, Caleb, Briana, Jorge, Maria . . . Connect with and guide them and build a team of "us" that embraces individuality and differences for the good of the company, not broadens the gap between "us" and "them."

Alex was just one shining example of something that happens to me every day in this millennial world. It's time to stop chasing relevance and make it happen to you.

Acknowledgments

Huge and bold thanks to . . .

Jim Eber: Without your patience, diligence, ear, and pen, we would not have captured every bit of our kick-ass message and great stories. You made us stronger, better, smarter, and more giving and empathetic than half-a-dozen shrinks with a side of Google could.

Stacey Sultar: You only garnered one reference in this book but are part of the soul and fabric of each page we created. Your steadfast and discerning passion to make something great shine through. Your friendship and support continue to push me to be the best coach, consultant, entrepreneur, empowerer, and person I want to be. We wrote, designed, developed, and published a great book.

Danielle Negroni: No words can express my gratitude for your partnership on this journey called life, paying the bills while I indulged in my zeal to create a book, company, message, and software business to pivot to my true love and gift—telling people what to do (LOL!) and providing better leadership, modernizing coaching, and influencing this amazing next generation. You are the ultimate combination of a great mom and a hot and fun wife!

Zach, Allie, and Matthew Negroni: You and 2.4 billion millennials worldwide are my reason for writing this book. Each of you has trained me, albeit differently, and prepared me to share the original gift of bold coaching with the world: parenting. Thank you for being my own special laboratory and tolerating my practicing on each of you. Each of you may be categorized as millennials, but you are really the next-generation leaders who will change the world.

Peter Negroni: Thanks for being kind, supportive, patient, wise, and my dad—I learned a lot.

Susan Levine: Thanks for being a loving and caring Mom.

Ann Rockeman: You could have run to the adjacent hills when I stalked you, convinced you to start a business to focus on millennials that integrates mind, body, and career, and helped develop Strength & Story out of a white-walled-and-floored straight-jacket room/ex-flower shop next to your wellness studio. You stayed, bought in, and even brought your business wife, **Vicki King**, to help, support, and devote herself to our cause and business. Vicki, you are another amazing and unexpected gift in this journey.

My Maximizers: Renee Schor, Marlene Taylor, Thad Kahlow, Sue Farrow, Cliff Boro, Chau Lai, Tyson McDowell, and Jon Hamby— all of you convinced me to stop attracting assholes, do my own thing, follow my own path, and become a true start-up CEO and entrepreneur. You stood by me, hired me, pimped me out, and listened to me whine and proselytize. You all wanted the book and here it is. You are all part of it in a special way.

Tyson MCDowell: You were my inspiration to really connect with brilliant millennials in my business and by guide in making launchbox a next generation software and app business.

Lauren Tanny: You encouraged me to live my dream while really, really making it about others.

Giles Raymond: Your encouragement, guidance, and listening have meant the world to me. Your perspective is super helpful, and the fact that I still get to work with you on a daily basis is a gift that keeps giving; you are a true Giving Leader. You even "gave" us your multitalented wife, **Antoinette Raymond**, whose energy and assistance in design of curriculum and spirit raised our bar to Bridge the Gap. Antoinette, we love you.

Jill Luedtke: Your friendship, support, faith, cheerleading, editing and design services, lending (with John) your own millennials as guinea pigs, sharing the joy of your family, and skiing not only have made a resounding impact on my life but they also made this book possible. You define what family is about.

The Ginsbergs and Berkovits: Thanks to each of you for being my family, loving me, treating me like your own, and being true mentors. And to **Erica Sweet**: what a journey—so glad you were part of mine!

Laura Morton: Without you there would be no book. Your hand-holding, calling us out, and helping, combined with your experience, connections, and energy, have helped me define our business, our offering, and our brand promise. Thank you for finding Jim and for your great and innovative mind. Thanks to **Laura** and **Brian Tauber** and **Cliff Boro** for the reintroduction to you.

Suzanne Fass: Your copyediting made this book a better book. It even got Stacey to realize I actually was vulnerable—not an easy feat. And **Jane Falla**, your proofreading and comments about the book made me know that we really have something special here and that we will change lives and create next-gen leaders.

Alyssa Pachiella: Your eye, design sense, and patience brought visual acuity to our business. Thank you for being you and for sharing your amazing talent and eye for telling our story through images. **Meghan Day Healey** of Story Horse: You took the proverbial ball when we needed you most and carried it across the finish line with aplomb. **Amy Beam**: Your empathetic and wonderful spirit and belief (not to mention that amazing laugh) have helped us deliver our message to the world.

Dr. Lorie Teagno: Your passion for helping others has defined my path, which all started with cleaning my side of the effin street and really finding myself.

Tracey Hornbuckle: You gave it your all and are the best cheerleader and dance partner a start-up CEO could have. You also wanted the book. Here it is!

Gabriella Hajdu: As my executive assistant and chief kick-my-butt person, you keep the bills paid and the lights on, you make sure everything works, and you regularly push yourself out of your comfort zone. **Mary Ann Daugherty and Bob Mowry**: Your dedication to spreading the word and working on business development has helped us spread the gospel.

Jim Walters: For teaching me, letting me share my thoughts, your leadership style, management ideas, and caring all boxed up in a real business. Out of all the mentors I had, you hold skills I admire: integrity, loyalty, patience, will, and bold caring. I can only hope to continue to be the leader you are.

Todd Salovey and Mitch Simon: You have given me a voice that delivers value, starts at the core heart, and makes it about others. You shared with me the secret about real communication.

Rob Peritz: You keep me in shape both mentally and physically. Our runs have been integral to creating launchbox, and your friendship and direct advice are second to none.

Justin Nahama, Joe Musselman, Phillip Dana, and The Honor Foundation: I am honored by the opportunity and experience to know, teach with, and be around you. And to all of The Honor Foundation fellows, past and present: Through your dedication to our country, and more importantly, for the vulnerability and strength that we have derived from having the honor to coach and connect each of you, your journeys make mine look like kindergarten.

Challenged Athletes Foundation: You changed lives by forcing me to change gears. My experiences through you have been some of the most formative in my life and have driven me to create a business that focuses on next-generation leadership.

To my original gangster clients (Mitch, Lillian, Thad, Trevor, Matt, Troy, Andy, Peter, Walt, Andrew, and Justin), friends, and coaches: You guys believed in us and the difference we could make in your businesses. You supported us while we supported you. I am at a loss for words (rare for me!) to express my appreciation. We look forward to many, many more times at bat.

And to every next-generation leader: Chase and find your relevance— it will pay off!

Notes on Sources

In the "B: Bust Myths" chapter, I cited these lines from the U.S. Chamber of Commerce Foundation's *Millennial Generation Research Review* (*bit.ly/1QAjTV9*): "Millennials are likely the most studied generation to date. . . . There are data to find pretty much whatever you are looking for, as the data are varied and sometimes contradictory. In fact, Millennials are full of contradictions, which, of course, may explain the youth of any generation." This is why, when it comes to millennial research, I don't think about the Socrates quote that started this book but a Greek myth: the legend of Sisyphus, whose name has become synonymous for endless tasks. It is a Sisyphean task to keep track of the endless stream of millennial statistics. So, for the book, I only quoted from books and essays (clearly credited throughout the book and not repeated here) as well as research from sources I trusted for their solid methodologies and deep data samples.

Introduction

The first set of bulleted statistics on retention comes from a survey of human resources professionals by Millennial Branding and Beyond.com titled, "The Cost of Millennial Retention." (*bit.ly/1hfaZSB*). The second set of statistics on disengagement comes from Gallup, which has been tracking the engagement levels of the US working population annually since 2000 (*bit.ly/1uUCjpX*). The final set of bullets comes from the most recent Pulse report by Greenfield Services Inc. (*bit.ly/21jQxpv*). The information on millennials living at home comes from the US Census Bureau, US Department of Education, and the Pew Research Center research found at *1.usa.gov/1CxxfO7* and *pewrsr.ch/1VNfQLa*, respectively. The statistics on whether millennials will live their dreams come from the "Millennial Disruption Index" prepared by Scratch, a Viacom Media Company. You can find many of these statistics cited by Anne Hubert in the YouTube video found at *http://bit.ly/1TKpNcW*. Spending reports for millennials vary widely. I used numbers from the Accenture study, "Who are the Millennial shoppers? And what do they *really* want?" (*http://bit.ly/1pgy7og*) and MarketingCharts' "How Much Influence Do Teens Wield Over Their Parents' Purchase Decisions?" (*http://bit.ly/212IEiw*).

Part One

In "Skills, Passions & Values," I cite Google's Project Oxygen and eight things great managers do, and then I ranked them in order of importance. This comes from *The New York Times* article, "Google's Quest to Build a Better Boss" (*nyti.ms/1TBejHu*), which is how Google promotes it on its own site. Interestingly, as this book went to press, Google released another survey through *The New York Times*, "What Google Learned from Its Quest to Build the Perfect Team" (*nyti.ms/20Vn3sz*). The article by Charles Duhigg cites that "new research reveals surprising truths about why some work groups thrive and others falter." I'm not sure how surprising this employee survey, called "Project Aristotle," will be to you after reading this book—not because it isn't excellent, but because it reinforces so much of what I wrote long before it came out. As Duhigg

writes, "Project Aristotle is a reminder that when companies try to opti-
mize everything, it's sometimes easy to forget that success is often built
on experiences — like emotional interactions and complicated conversations and discussions of who we want to be and how our teammates
make us feel — that can't really be optimized." The Zappos Family Core
Values can be found here: *bit.ly/1PhFp2F*. The Seth Godin quote that starts
the "Story" chapter is actually from his terrific blog (*bit.ly/1lhNGVV*). The
stats from the disruption index in the same chapter are from Innosight
(*bit.ly/1y5Srfo*).

Part Two

In "B: Bust Myths," I used The Center for Creative Leadership study (*bit
.ly/1WLLg3f*), data from a great article in *The Economist* (*econ.st/1H7JkZ9*),
and Future Workplace's "Multiple Generations @ Work" (*bit.ly/1FJf5It*).
At the start of "D: Deliver Value," I cite statistics from the Steelcase
privacy survey (*bit.ly/1WLMrj6*), the Pew Research Center's updated
survey on text messaging (*pewrsr.ch/1KO8apS*), and the most recent data
on word consumption, which has only grown (*bit.ly/1WLN8ZL*). You
can read *The New York Times* story quoted in "E: Empowerment" here
(*nyti.ms/1JSm1EJ*) and listen to the NPR story here (*n.pr/1LJqiRU*).

About launchbox

We help individuals and organizations achieve BOLD results by creating next-generation leaders and bridging the gap between millennials and non-millennials to create real-deal relationships.

For Organizations

We help create authentic, powerful, and connected workplaces, delivering value through

- workplace assessments
- customized workshops
- speaking engagements
- one-on-one coaching
- online services and enterprise software solutions
- consulting, advising, and research on the next generation

Our goal is to help organizations win with their people and clients/customers by

- attracting and retaining the right employees
- creating bold leadership
- building open, collaborative cultures
- developing connected, motivated teams that work together to achieve and sustain high performance and profits
- driving increased engagement, productivity, and profits in the workplace
- building brand connections, loyalty, and revenue in the marketplace

For Millennials

We love and understand millennials. We help them kick more ass for themselves and the people and companies they work for through

- workshops focused on understanding their strengths, skills, values, and passions; developing their personal brands; and delivering their stories
- peer-to-peer networking groups
- customized coaching services
- online services and apps

Our goal is to empower millennials win in their personal and professional lives by

- defining who they are, what they want to do, and how to get there
- growing personally and professionally
- enhancing their careers: getting the right jobs, promotions, and capabilities
- developing professional networks
- generating new business
- improving relationships and work/life balance

858.314.9867 | www.**launchbox365**.com

Index